Crafts Activities

Featuring 65 Holiday Ideas

Crafts Activities

Featuring 65 Holiday Ideas

Carl E. Frankson
Kenneth R. Benson

Grace E. Gluck
Illustrator

Parker Publishing Company, Inc.
West Nyack, New York

© 1970, by
PARKER PUBLISHING COMPANY, INC.
West Nyack, New York

Library of Congress
Catalog Card Number: 77-98386

PRINTED IN THE UNITED STATES OF AMERICA
B & P   13-188755-6

Affectionately Dedicated to
Bernice and Evelyn
whose inspiration and help greatly contributed
to the contents of this book.

INTRODUCTION

This book was written with the understanding that crafts and crafts activities play an extremely important role in the development of children. The manipulative experience, so provided, combines the whole of the child as he conceptualizes ideas and has the opportunity to execute them in project form. This combination of utilizing the normal desire for children to create with the more academic type of learning, presents a composite rather than segmented learning experience. The understandings are greatly enhanced through the visual, particularly when the youngster has been a part of the total created project. The three-dimensional item has far greater meaning than merely the rote memorization of factual information. Children, by their very nature, are dynamic and vibrant and wish to express in more concrete forms their inter-sensitivities. It is logical for educators to capitalize upon these characteristics in order to more effectively provide educational and recreational experiences during the educative process. It is with these thoughts in mind that CRAFTS ACTIVITIES has been developed. Out of these diversified projects, teachers can select those experiences for children that will fit the particular unit, or units, of academic learning for more effective instruction.

The special holidays activities section at the end of the book has been organized according to some of the recognized major holidays of the year. Research conducted on a national scale concerning the needs of teachers in these areas has been the principle guide lines for the development of this section. Each holiday has a one page explanation of the general significance that the teacher may wish to use in her presentations. The explanations of the significance of the holiday is followed by project ideas that can in all instances be modified to meet the individual requirements of a particular class. While some of these holidays contain more ideas than others, this seeming dichotomy is a result of research with teachers and their felt needs for a particular holiday to have a wider selection than others. This does not mean to infer that some are more important than others, but rather what teachers have requested as an assist in their programs.

Carl E. Frankson
Kenneth R. Benson

REALISTIC LEARNING THROUGH CRAFTS

Tools, materials and manipulative skills contribute greatly to the total integrated learning for children. During this early developmental period of life when a child is attempting to find his individual identity, meaningful and productive experiences are crucial if the child is expected to enter adulthood with a broad background upon which to build. During these experiences children have an opportunity to make direct judgments. Virtually immediately they can ascertain the validity of their reasoning as they construct two- or three-dimensional projects.

The results of their judgments are obvious in the partially or fully completed projects. They, therefore, have a personal opportunity to evaluate their success based upon their developed skills. These meaningful activities involving motor skills set early patterns of understanding so necessary for more complicated theoretical and symbolic learning.

The educative process has been based over the years on almost a tunnel vision concept where only a small segment of a youngster's genetic proclivities are utilized and commented upon. The child that has had early understanding and symbolic learning, i.e., the ability to read and understand symbols, achieves early successes while others not so endowed meet fundamental failures. It is hoped that teachers and leaders of children begin to recognize, to a far greater extent than they have in the past, that basic simple and uncomplicated manipulative experiences are fundamental to education and contribute to the joy of learning.

Children live in a three-dimensional world exposed to thousands of influences both good and bad and it is up to those who are in leadership roles in the educative process to bring with forceful vigor varied experiences that graphically illustrate those things that are verbally discussed. It is unreasonable to expect a child to know the difference between such words as sharp and dull, unless he has had personalized contact with the edge of a piece of metal as opposed to the flat surface of the same piece of metal. How can we further expect a youngster to understand the difference between a drab, dull color as opposed to the sharp brightness of cardinal red. These and thousands of other experiences are within the grasp of children when the teacher provides suitable opportunities for direct and enhanced learning opportunities. Children by their very nature thoroughly enjoy these types of creative activities. They enter into them as a part of their natural emotional development. To the child, this experimentation, explanation and self-knowledge are all concomitants in this educational play activity. As youngsters develop greater skill and emotional stability, and as their interest span increases, the experienced teacher will bring them into a more structured type of program that more clearly relates to these symbolic learning skills. The early entrance of children into these activities is of extreme importance and experimentation should be extensively encouraged at this time. This experimentation phase should utilize a wide variety of media including crayons, paper, magic markers, tempera paints and plasticine and other (free) types of materials.

These unstructured experiences should be encouraged and recognized as an essential aspect of the total learning process.

Intellectual curiosity can be encouraged by having two or three dimensional items that have been self-created and upon which a child can focus as a result of direct contact. Creativity can be developed through challenges in the performance of varied craft activities. Youngsters are not stimulated by experiences which are too simple for them; however, interest for them is quickly destroyed if the activity is not clearly understood or is too complicated.

Interest spans among children vary greatly; therefore, the project challenges should be varied as well as the completion times. One of the basic aims is to develop such an interest span that attention also increases. It is psychologically unwise to create conditions that give instantaneous success. Children will recognize under these conditions that they have contributed very little. However, given the proper stimulus, a great deal of the youngsters' ingenuity will flow out and indeed become part of "their projects."

All children need some direction in their work. This assistance, which is rendered through suggestions and explanations, should be fairly brief and within the youngsters' understanding. Frequently, questions such as, "What does this remind you of?" "What do you think you see?" and "Do you like what you see?" assists in soliciting ideas that can be used in the future. This verbalization on the part of the child focuses his attention on what he has done and what he is about to do. It also contributes much to the development of observative powers often times taken for granted. These experiences give children much in the way of opportunity in the development of language facilities and assists in gradually building their confidence in themselves.

MATERIALS NEEDED FOR CRAFTS PROGRAMS

Brightly colored construction papers are used in many of the projects. Heavier poster paper and various weights of cardboard along with colored tissue and crepe paper are also desirable. A generous supply of newspaper and paper towels will add utility to your paper supply. Tracing paper and carbon paper for transfer of ideas will be most useful.

Soft lead pencils, well sharpened and placed in a suitable container along with a generous supply of colored crayons will be very useful. Do not discard short lengths of crayons as they can be used for crayon rubbings and other activities. Crayons should be kept away from the heat of the sun. Valuable additions and virtually indispensable in craft activities are marking pens, both felt and nylon tipped. These pens come in many colors as well as line width sizes. Be certain that these pens are capped when not in use, as they dry out quickly.

A wide variety of paints are desirable to have on hand to implement the finishing of projects. Generally, poster or tempera paints can be purchased ready mixed in jars. They have a bright intensity of color. Water colors come in little cakes or tubes and are useful in picture painting as a paint wash.

Acrylic paints are also water based and come in tubes. They dry very rapidly. Brushes used for these paints should be washed immediately after being used. The acrylic paints dry with a dull finish. A polymer medium can be applied directly over these paints. It is a colorless liquid that is brushed over the paint. Oil based paints are thinned with turpentine and brushes are cleaned in kerosene or turpentine. Care should be exercised in the use of all paints, particularly oil based and lacquer based paints. These paints are difficult to remove from clothing as some synthetic fabrics will be dissolved by the solvent used in laquer paints. It is also important to remind teachers that a youngster's skin is soft and tender and may react to solvents such as turpentine and lacquer. It is more desirable to permit small amounts of paint to remain on a child's hand than to vigorously scrub with turpentine which frequently results in a turpentine burn. The key is in precaution in the use of paint and paint products. Under no circumstances should lead based paints be used in these activities.

Paint brushes came in assorted sizes and shapes. While it is recognized that good brushes, such as camels hair, will last longer and will produce better results, it is hard to justify this expense particularly when these items, even after extreme care is exercised in their use, become broken or damaged. In all instances brushes should be cleaned immediately after use and should be stored flat. They should never be stored in the paint jars.

Adhesives, glues, pastes and tapes are essential items for your crafts program. Rubber cement is an ideal adhesive. Be certain to apply a thin coating to each surface to be adhered. Permit to dry. When thoroughly dry, press firmly together. This gluing process reduces the necessity to hold the materials together until the glue is dry. Rubber cement works only on porous materials; for non-porous materials such as metal, Duco cement should be used. It should be recognized that this cement is almost impossible to remove from fabrics. One of the best all around adhesives is a white glue that comes in various forms and is water soluble. Library paste also works extremely well on paper. Masking tape and Scotch tape can contribute much to the problem of fastening units together. Colored tapes not only contribute to the problem of fastening units together, but also provide ornamentation and design for the finished product.

Scissors and knives and other cutting tools should always be kept in a sharpened condition. However, blunt scissors are a must for young children. Craft knives that have removable blades are recommended for use by older children. Tables should be protected with heavy cardboard when knives are used in cutting out stencils and the like.

Additional equipment that is recommended should include a paper punch, pencil compass, a rule, and a stapler. A stapler can be an accident hazard if not properly demonstrated. Teachers are cautioned that youngsters have a tendency to place fingers between the anvil and the actuating arm that may result in a well stapled finger rather than a carefully stapled project.

ORGANIZING FOR CRAFTS ACTIVITIES

It is generally recognized that manipulative craft experiences for children contain four individual, yet connected, segments. These segments are (1) the conceptionalization of the idea, (2) organizing for the activity, (3) the construction of the item or items and (4) the clean-up associated with the activity.

Craft activities should be organized around a central theme of academic work, frequently around a significant holiday area such as Christmas, Hanukkah or Thanksgiving, so that the study of the significance of the event is enhanced by the creation of a two or three dimensional project. Great insight and understandings into the individual child oftentimes results from such questions as "Why did you choose to do this particular project?" or "Where did you get the idea?" These questions, and similar ones, lead into verbal responses on the part of the child. He verbalizes not only as a result of the question, but has a tendency to put into words a meaning that has been triggered by his tactile experiences. It is imperative that a child be provided the opportunity to conceptualize within the framework of the particular idea.

The organization of the classroom for the activity should take into account that the child must also learn how to organize for himself the procedures necessary for a successful experience. He should begin to understand that certain fundamental processes must occur in an organized and sequential pattern. For example, if a youngster is creating a wooden Viking ship for the study of exploration, it is far more effective to sand smooth each part prior to assembly, rather than attempting to sand after all the pieces have been fastened together. The exuberancy of children and their desire to complete a project quickly, requires astute leadership on the part of the teachers to prevent hurried and "sloppy" craftsmanship. A fine balance between excessive standards of excellence and slovenly work should be developed. Children's interest spans are generally short. Frequently, they parallel the honey bee as it flitters from flower to flower. Youngsters have a tendency to go from one thing to another very frequently. Teachers are well aware of this and should try to prevent children from attempting things that are exceedingly difficult with little chance that the youngster will be able to complete his project.

During the construction of the item or items, because of the interest spans involved, manipulative experiences should be of fairly short duration and at times when academic learning seems to have reached a particular plateau, or has become trying. Class restlessness may be one of the indications that a more physical activity is needed. During the construction it is desirable for youngsters to work in small groups, thereby creating a further enhancement and extension of the original idea as concepts are gleaned from one another. Cooperation between students is a concomitant learning experience when children assist one another in such activities as holding, gluing or pasting. Youngsters working in small groups have the ready resources within the group for that extra pair of hands.

At the termination of the activity for the day, each child should be held responsible for his particular area. This includes his desk, or table, and adjacent floor area. Brushes should be cleaned and all tools and materials should be returned to their proper places. One or two youngsters should be designated for each central area to be certain that the tools have been returned to their proper places, and materials have been properly sealed. Finished and unfinished projects clearly marked by the child's name should be placed on their designated shelves. Until all these tasks have been performed satisfactorily, the teacher should not move to the next segment of the day's learning experience.

The teacher who fails to recognize the place of each of these segments, is failing to provide a full and total experience for children. It should also be stated at this point that failure to effectively organize with these essential segments in mind, not only leads to confusion within the classroom structure, but also contributes to the lack of organized thinking on the part of participants. Orderliness on the part of children as they participate is not a deterrent to creativity, but develops to a much higher degree the analytical approach to doing. In addition, orderliness of procedure establishes a higher degree of desire on the part of teachers, not only to permit but to encourage students to engage in these manipulative experiences that are genuine concomitants to academic learning. Far too frequently teachers shy away from craft activities in the classroom because they are "too messy." Literally, the educative process should provide opportunity for total experiences in order that a youngster has maximum growth. The development on the part of the teacher in establishing a standardized modus-operandi increases the desire to participate.

There is hardly anything more frustrating than to expend exuberancy by looking for needed tools, supplies and equipment because no standardized places have been established for storing these implements of learning. In our own homes we have established rather precise places where one locates essentials such as glasses, cups, saucers, and other necessary items for day to day living.

How frustrating it is to have to search out obscure hiding places for scissors, knives, and adhesives. Frequently the level of frustration is so great among children that they will retreat from their original creative idea into a more standardized pattern because of their inability to locate needed items.

This retreat solidifies in the mind of the child the seeming desirability of conforming rather than exploring. The youngster feels that exploring is far too much of a frustrating experience and, therefore, he begins to form, early in life, a pattern of conformity. It should also be stated that well organized activities place far less of a strain on the teacher as she now can spend her valuable time in instruction of students rather than being essentially a procurer of supplies. Our home experiences in living with children prompts us to remember the countless number of times when they ask their parents to find shoes, raincoats and books. Multiply this request by the average class size of approximately thirty. During manipulative experiences and without specific organization, the teacher will be merely a dispenser of supplies with little opportunity to teach. Small individual boxes that contain frequently used items such as scissors, knives, coping saws, nails, brads and such measuring devices as rules, are essential for a well organized program. It is also desirable to paint each box a distinctive color with a silhouette of the item painted or stenciled on top, thereby making it easy to recognize.

A discarded chest of drawers, gaily decorated, can provide excellent housing for construction paper, boxes, papers, masking tape and fabric remnants. A vented small metal cabinet can be used to store volatile paints and finishing materials such as shellac, lacquer, and oil based paints. The respective solvents for these materials should also be kept in sealed containers in these cabinets. In short, organize well for maximum outcomes.

SPECIAL TECHNIQUES IN CRAFTS

RUBBER CEMENT

When using rubber cement, coat each surface that is to be used and permit to dry. Then place coated surfaces together and press.

PLASTER OF PARIS

Fill mixing container approximately half full with water when mixing plaster of Paris. Slowly sprinkle the plaster of Paris into the water—do not stir. When the entire surface of water is covered with a thin film of dry plaster, wait several minutes, then slowly stir the mixture. If you experience too rapid a setting, the next time you mix add a talblespoon of vinegar to each pint of water used. To determine how much water to begin with, fill the mold with water and this will provide enough mixture with a little left over to complete your requirements. Paint the object using tempera paints.

Verniculite can be added to plaster of Paris when mixed with water to create carving blocks. This additive improves the carving characteristics of the material.

CHALK DRAWING

To make chalk drawings more permeable, coat the paper with skim milk. Apply the chalk when wet. After the paper dries, the chalk will not brush off. If it is desirable to work with the paper dry, the colored chalks can be set by spraying with clear lacquer or hair spray.

PAINTING WAXED CARTONS

Waxed cartons can be painted by adding liquid soap to tempera paints. To increase the permanency, spray with clear lacquer.

VEGETABLE DYES

Vegetable dyes are non-toxic, yet very effective coloring agents for textiles, woods and other open grained materials.

LACQUER PAINTS AND SPRAYS

Lacquer sprays or paints should never be applied over oil based paints as they will act as a paint remover and destroy the smooth finish of the original object.

SAWDUST MODELING MATERIALS

Sawdust and glue mixed together make a desirable modeling material. It is suggested that water soluable glue be used.

MODELING FORMULA FOR BEADS

To make paper beads, dissolve one heaping tablespoon of corn starch into a small amount of water. Add one cup of boiling water and one-fourth cup of salt. Boil until clear, add one cup of shredded newspaper and stir. Boil about ten minutes. Remove from stove and let the material cool. Mold into beads. Holes for the thread are made with a needle. Permit to dry and string. Beads may be colored by using tempera paints prior to spraying with clear lacquer.

PAPIER MÂCHÉ

If the project calls for papier mâché, it may be made by adding equal parts of plaster of Paris and asbestos. Add water and mix to a putty like consistency. Let dry and paint.

MAKING RELIEF MAPS

Relief maps and terrains may be developed by using one pint of sawdust, one pint of plaster of Paris and one-third pint of soluble paste. Thin out the paste with water adding plaster of Paris first and then sawdust. Knead to a doughy consistency. This mixture will harden in approximately twenty minutes. If more time is desired for hardening, add a tablespoon full of vinegar.

SHOE POLISH

Shoe polish is an excellent coloring agent for wood and other porous materials.

GETTING STARTED

Teachers recognize the importance of effective personnel and class organization prior to launching a new unit or activity. In the crafts it is essential that children's clothing is properly protected. Each child should be asked to provide himself with an apron or simple smock. Frequently one of dad's old shirts with the sleeves cut off is placed on the child with the buttons up the back. Sometimes it is desirable to cut the collar from the shirt giving the child more freedom of movement. Children should be encouraged to work with clean hands as smudges from dirty hands quickly destroy the utility of a new piece of paper or similar material.

Encourage children to organize their work place with a suitable covering to prevent soiling the desk or table. A plastic sheet, or several layers of newspaper should be used to cover the working surface. If cutting is to be done, heavy cardboard should be placed under the items to be cut.

It is desirable to get together whatever items you may need before you start. It is essential to remember that the patterns of operations that you begin with are the ones that children will retain and continue with; therefore, it is highly recommended that these organizational patterns be thought out and meticulously followed so that children develop a modus-operandi conducive to the best of habit patterns.

Each child may well be equipped with a shoe box or other suitable container to hold the materials he is using. This organization makes for easy dispersal of a child's own crafts supplies. At the conclusion, smocks, aprons and materials should be carefully put away and the work area cleaned up and the child's hands should be washed.

CONTENTS

Holiday Craft Activities

OUT OF THE PAST

Use a large pine cone and attach an acorn to the narrow end with glue. Paint features on to the acorn and cut tail from construction paper, as well as front and hind legs. Attach legs and tail as illustrated using glue. Tapered paper cups may be used as a substitute for pine cones. Decorate with paint as desired.

BEAKS AND BILLS

This mobile lends itself extensively to the imagination of the process of balance.
Cut from construction paper or white drawing paper and enhance with the use of
colored felt marking pens. Participants can maufacture their own birds.

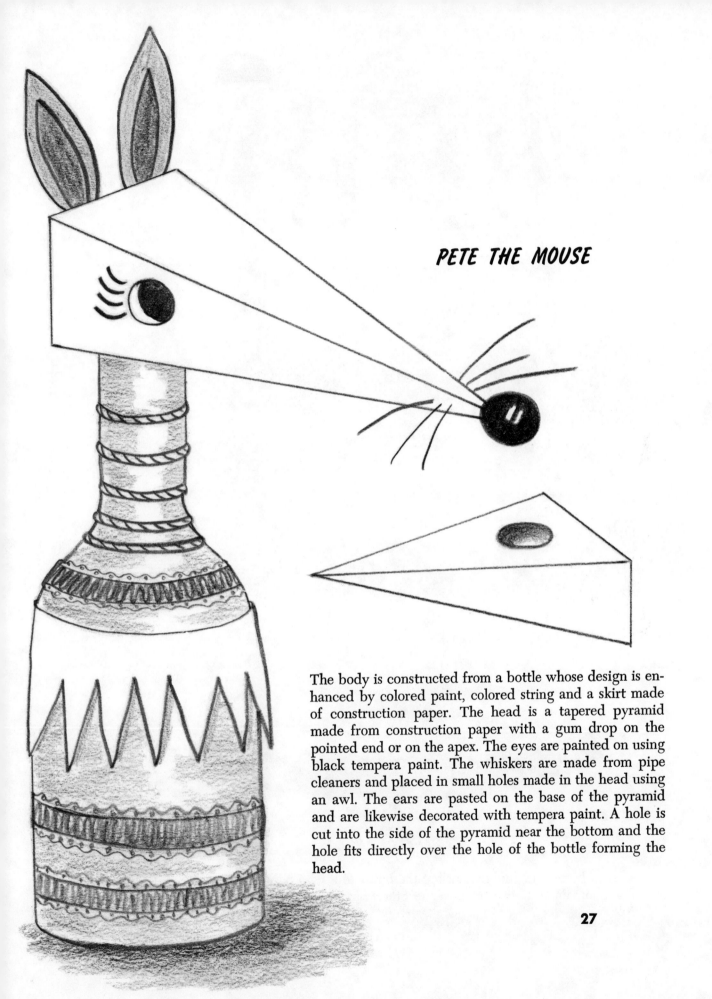

PETE THE MOUSE

The body is constructed from a bottle whose design is enhanced by colored paint, colored string and a skirt made of construction paper. The head is a tapered pyramid made from construction paper with a gum drop on the pointed end or on the apex. The eyes are painted on using black tempera paint. The whiskers are made from pipe cleaners and placed in small holes made in the head using an awl. The ears are pasted on the base of the pyramid and are likewise decorated with tempera paint. A hole is cut into the side of the pyramid near the bottom and the hole fits directly over the hole of the bottle forming the head.

27

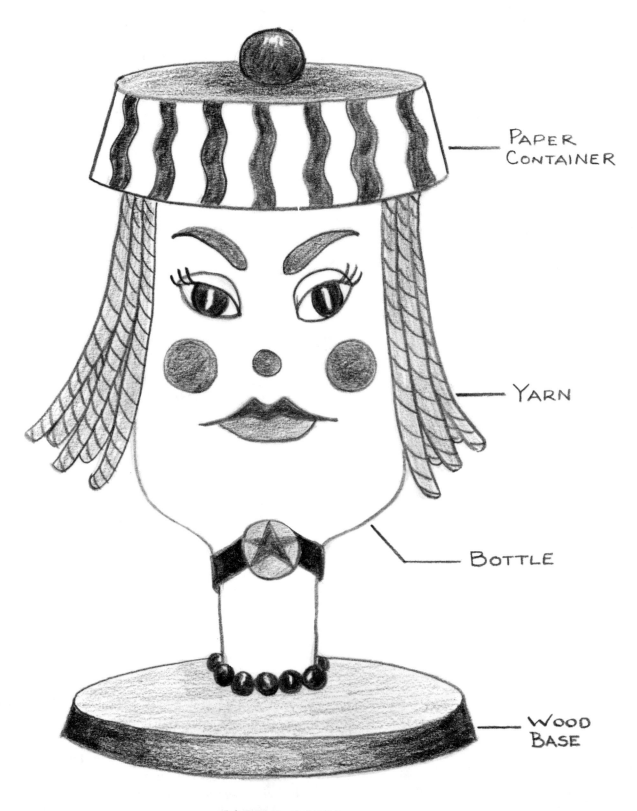

PAPER
CONTAINER

YARN

BOTTLE

WOOD
BASE

BOTTLE FACES

Invert a bottle and glue the neck of the bottle to a solid base. As a cap or hat use a paper container or strips of paper or other material such as yarn. Decorate as desired.

KITCHEN KRAFTS

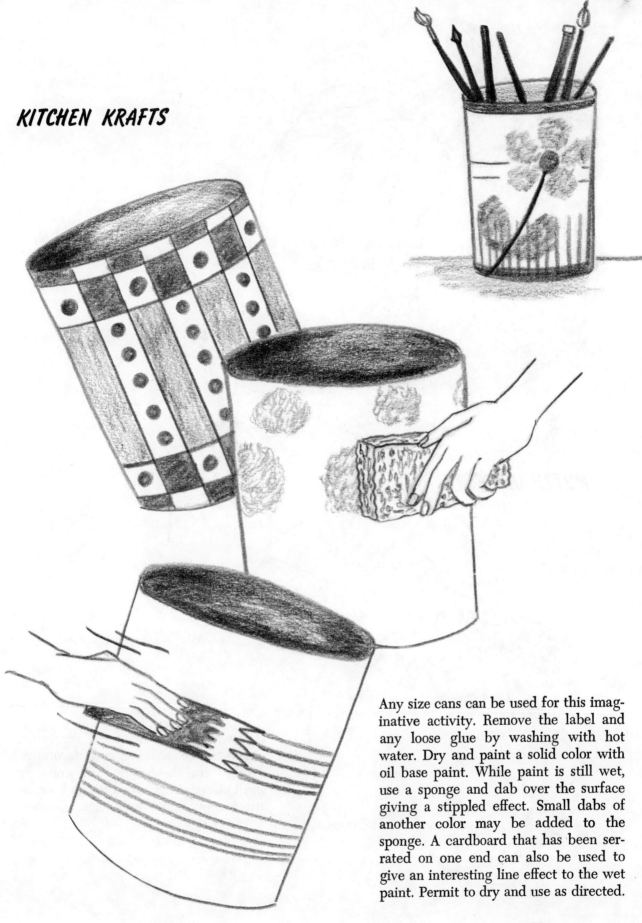

Any size cans can be used for this imaginative activity. Remove the label and any loose glue by washing with hot water. Dry and paint a solid color with oil base paint. While paint is still wet, use a sponge and dab over the surface giving a stippled effect. Small dabs of another color may be added to the sponge. A cardboard that has been serrated on one end can also be used to give an interesting line effect to the wet paint. Permit to dry and use as directed.

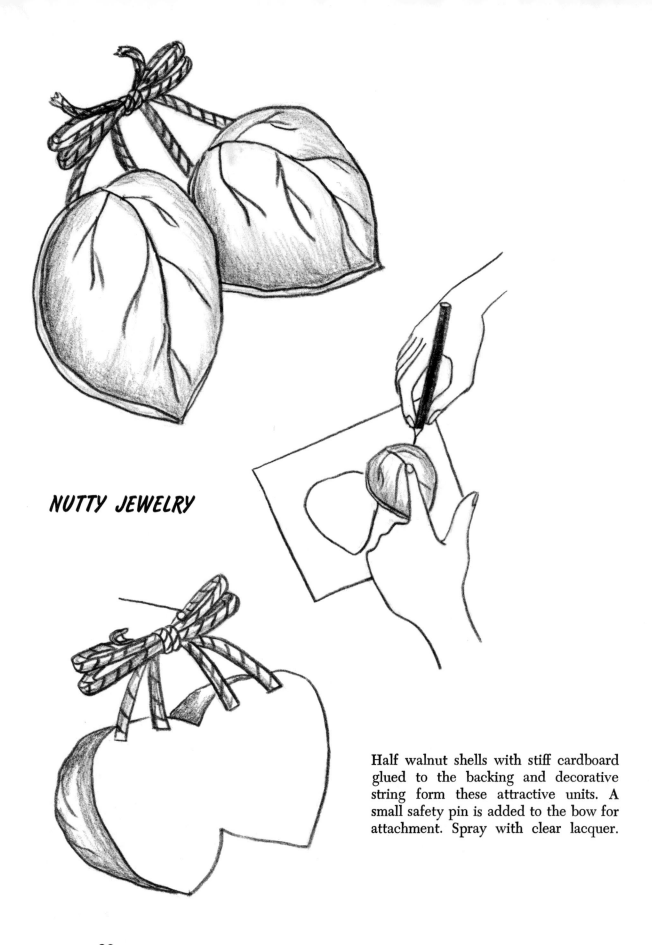

NUTTY JEWELRY

Half walnut shells with stiff cardboard glued to the backing and decorative string form these attractive units. A small safety pin is added to the bow for attachment. Spray with clear lacquer.

JOLLY ROGER AND GOOD GUYS, TOO

Take half a walnut shell with a small amount of plasticine forced into the bottom. The masts are constructed from toothpicks and are stuck in an upright position in the plasticine. The sails are from construction paper. Pennants are made from white drawing paper. Decorate as desired. Other shells can be used in a similar fashion.

MILK CARTON HOMES

A two quart milk container is an ideal size for our season visitors. For wrens an inch hole is cut into the side approximately two inches from the bottom. The perch is constructed from the side of another container. It is stapled or stitched on as illustrated. Two holes are punched in the top for hanging. The container can be decorated using casine paints.

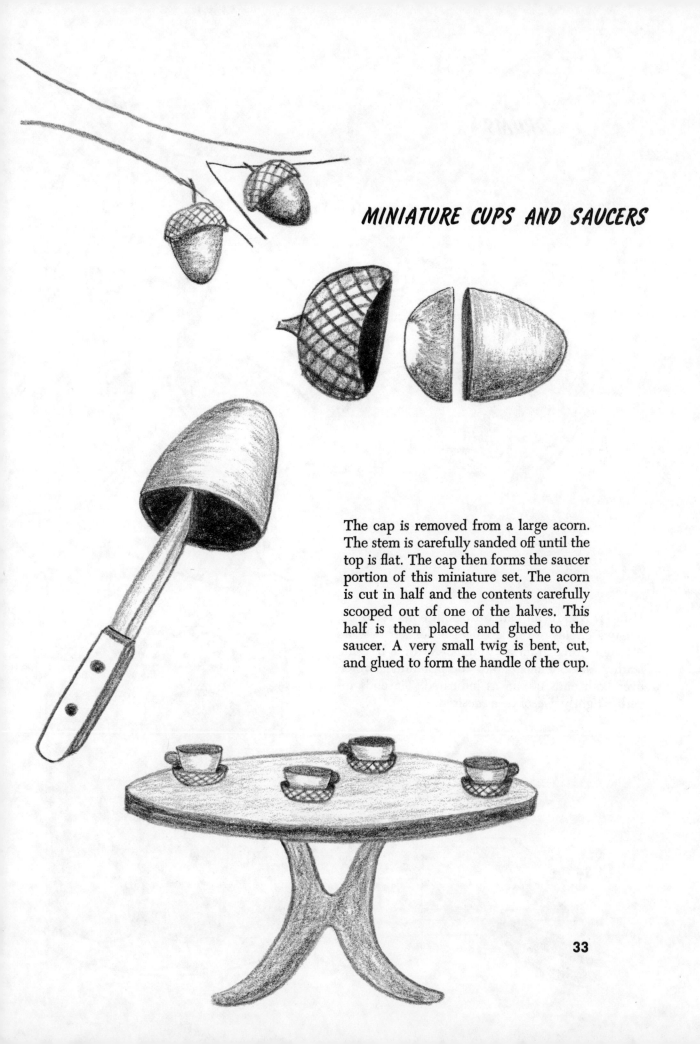

MINIATURE CUPS AND SAUCERS

The cap is removed from a large acorn. The stem is carefully sanded off until the top is flat. The cap then forms the saucer portion of this miniature set. The acorn is cut in half and the contents carefully scooped out of one of the halves. This half is then placed and glued to the saucer. A very small twig is bent, cut, and glued to form the handle of the cup.

33

DRUMS

DRUM HEAD

Using a No. 10 tin can with both ends removed, cut two circles of rubber sheet or leather. Use an old inner tube from an automobile tire. If using leather, soak. Punch holes for fastening, stretch over both ends of can as indicated. Tie ends together tightly. Decorate as desired.

34

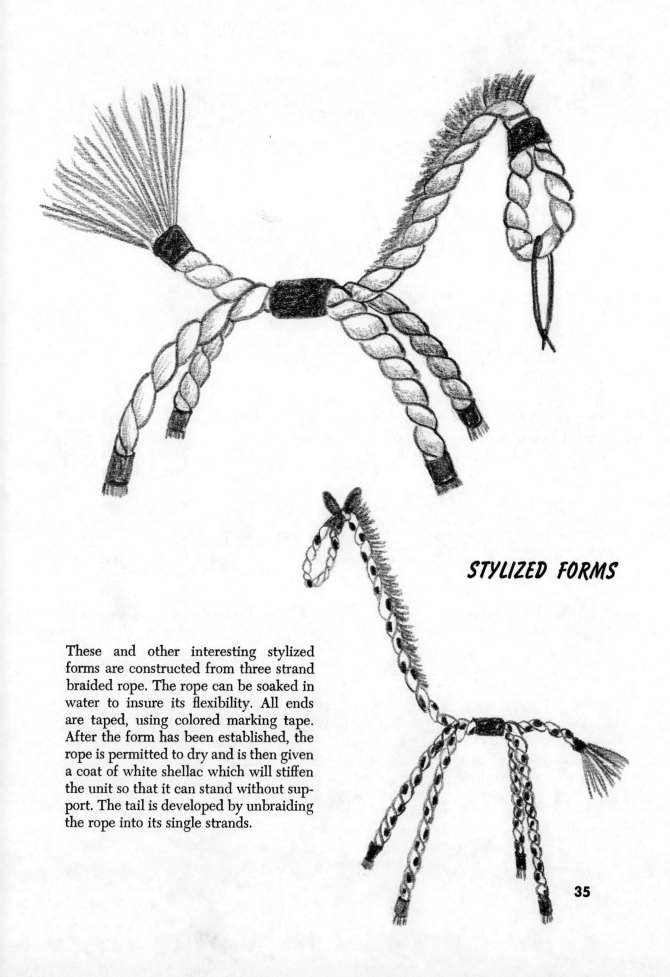

STYLIZED FORMS

These and other interesting stylized forms are constructed from three strand braided rope. The rope can be soaked in water to insure its flexibility. All ends are taped, using colored marking tape. After the form has been established, the rope is permitted to dry and is then given a coat of white shellac which will stiffen the unit so that it can stand without support. The tail is developed by unbraiding the rope into its single strands.

Measure size of head with thin strip of construction paper. Allow ½″ overlap for gluing. Design crown and cut out, glue ends together. Paint, add sequins, buttons, and the like as desired.

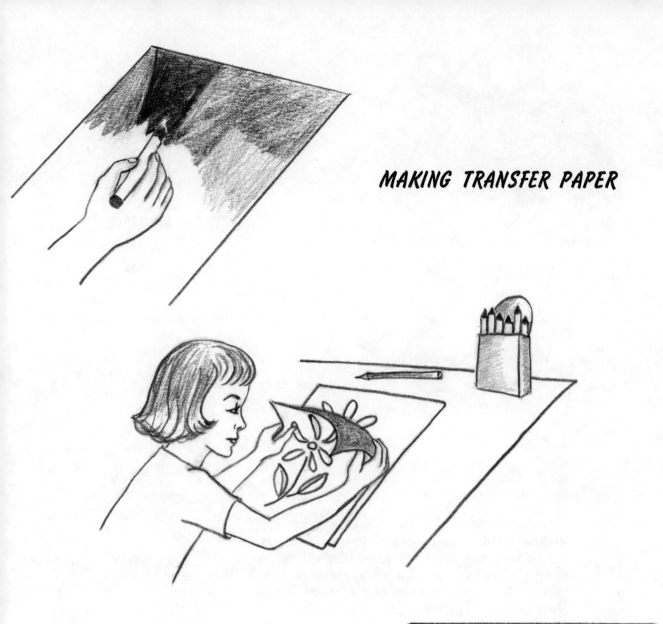

MAKING TRANSFER PAPER

Color all of one side of a sheet of typing paper very heavily with various colored crayons. Place paper with crayon side down on top of another sheet of typing paper. Use a ball point pen to develop a design. The design will be transferred to the bottom sheet.

37

SCRAP BOOK

Cut several pieces of construction paper into the desired size of your notebook. From old magazines, cut out selected colored pictures that will fit on the pages you have cut. Use paper cement to paste them to the pages. Use pen or crayons to design the title sheet. Punch holes as shown in the drawing and insert rings or colored string to complete the notebook.

WONDERFUL BRACELETS

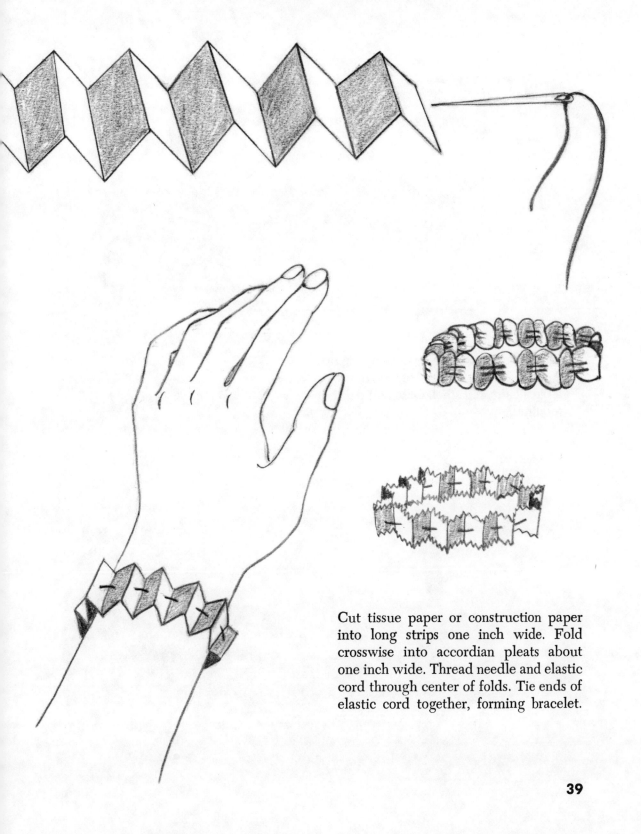

Cut tissue paper or construction paper into long strips one inch wide. Fold crosswise into accordian pleats about one inch wide. Thread needle and elastic cord through center of folds. Tie ends of elastic cord together, forming bracelet.

FURNITURE

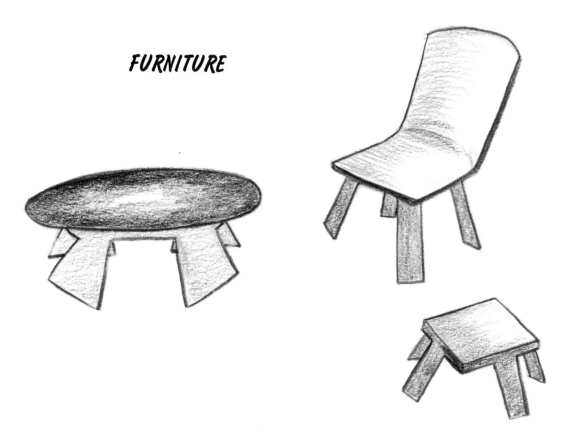

Using sharp knife and pointed scissors, cut molded egg carton into sections for table, chairs and stool. Glue and paint as required.

PRINTING FOR FUN

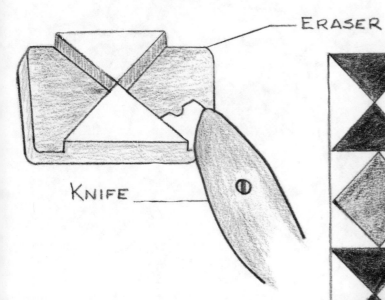

ERASER

KNIFE

Printing with small firm items such as erasers, cardboard strips, sponges, jar lids, cords and small blocks of wood, brush paints on items named and press the painted side on sheet of scrap paper. If satisfactory, print on good paper.

On white drawing paper, youngster draws a web, using black ink and lettering pen, or nylon marking pen. Insects are then drawn on web. Try creating your own insects.

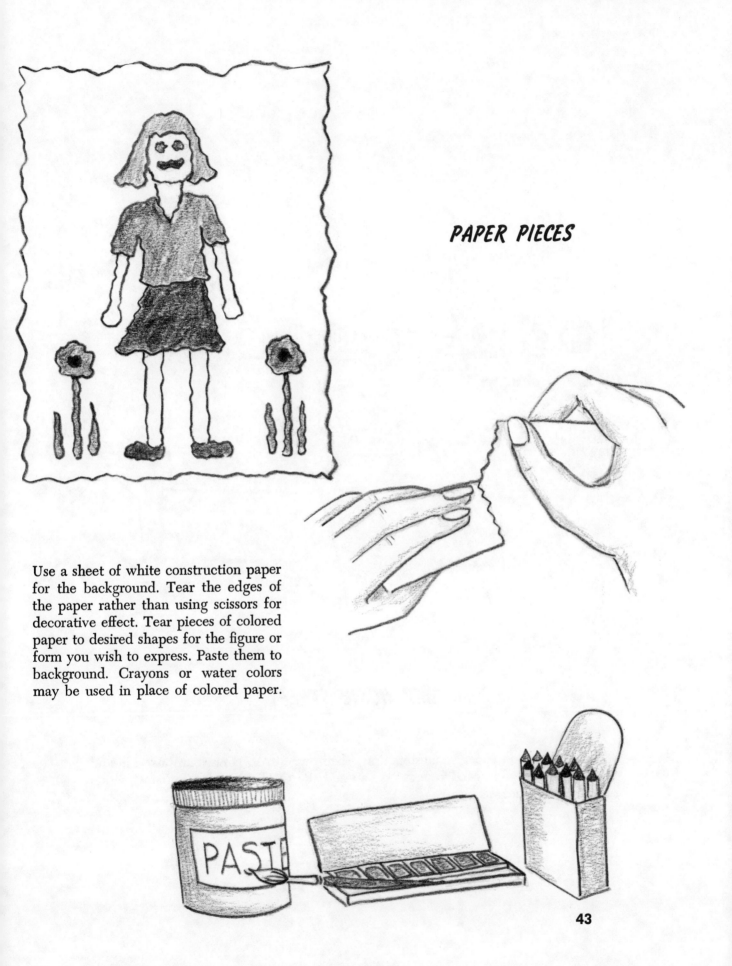

PAPER PIECES

Use a sheet of white construction paper for the background. Tear the edges of the paper rather than using scissors for decorative effect. Tear pieces of colored paper to desired shapes for the figure or form you wish to express. Paste them to background. Crayons or water colors may be used in place of colored paper.

MY HOME STREET

On construction paper youngsters draw their own street. Houses are inked in and colored. More advanced youngsters can add the third dimension by construction of their own house.

NATURE PICTURES

Cut out frame for picture from construction paper. Cut two sheets of wax paper slightly smaller than the outer dimension of the frame. Youngster uses pre-pressed leaves, ferns, grasses or flowers—arranged flat on one sheet of wax paper. Sprinkle crayon shavings around the assembled items. Cover with second piece of wax paper and press with warm flat iron. Mount with paste to frame.

45

Paint features on peanuts. Add sequins, hats, pipe cleaners, and so on, as desired to make your group. Can be mounted on wire and fastened to base.

WINTER FACES

Styrofoam balls, pins, sequins, buttons and your imagination add to these festive faces. Toothpicks form the three legs. Add your own ideas.

47

3-D PICTURES

Use half a plastic container for a flowerpot and glue to stiff cardboard. Each
stem is a heavy ink line, leaves and
flower petals have been colored and
pasted to cardboard. Flower center is
a button or bottle cap.

48

PAPER BAG MARIONETTES

Fill small paper bags with wads of newspaper. With string, tie top together. Glue on features that have been cut from construction paper. Cut four strips of construction paper ½ inch wide and eighteen inches long for the arms. Cement the two pieces together at the ends. Fold over one another the entire length and glue ends together. Repeat for other arm. Cut four strips one inch wide and eighteen inches long for legs. Glue and fold each piece the same way as for the arms. Glue in place as illustrated. Cut ears and glue on, cut out hands and feet and cement to arms and legs. String is adhered behind ears for control and use.

49

DANGLING PLANTER

Use half of a coconut that has been sanded. To suspend the flowerpot, drill three or four holes approximately ¼ inch from the rim and attach cord or heavy string. To the sides of the coconut fasten spiral seashells. Complete the flowerpot by inserting artificial or real flowers.

50

Select two fruit juice cans to be used as telephones. In the bottom of each of the cans drill or punch holes. Insert a string in each of these holes and tie on the inside of the can. Decorate the containers with paint or other materials. Holding string taut and alternately speaking and listening, one's voice can be heard over distances of hundreds of feet.

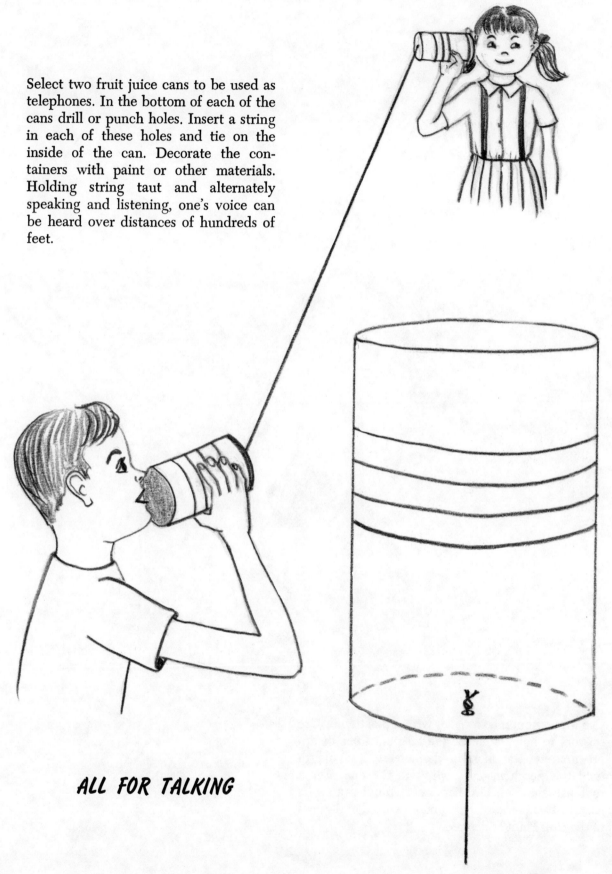

ALL FOR TALKING

WELCOME WRENS

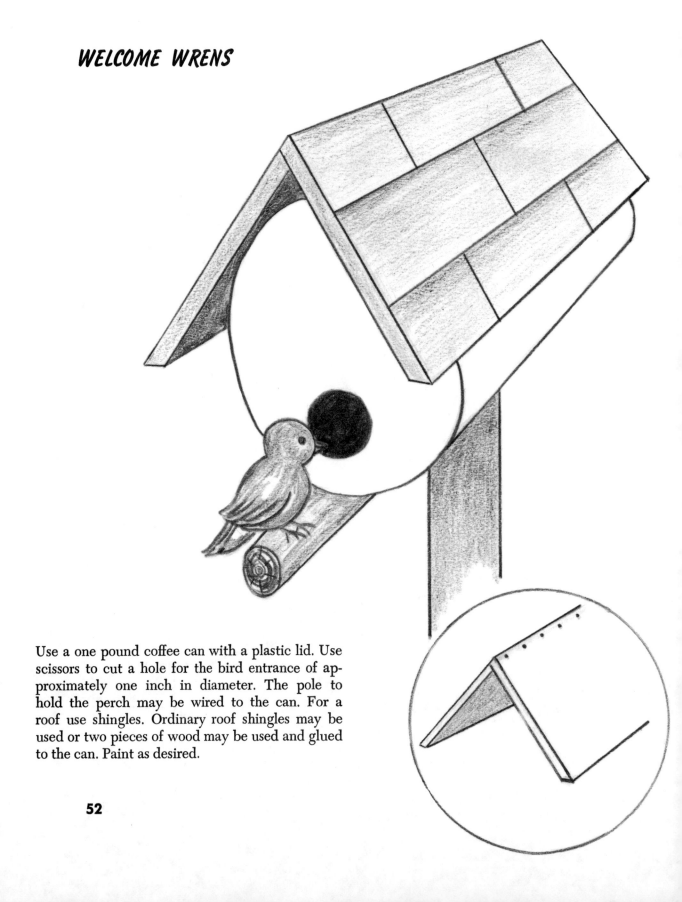

Use a one pound coffee can with a plastic lid. Use scissors to cut a hole for the bird entrance of approximately one inch in diameter. The pole to hold the perch may be wired to the can. For a roof use shingles. Ordinary roof shingles may be used or two pieces of wood may be used and glued to the can. Paint as desired.

52

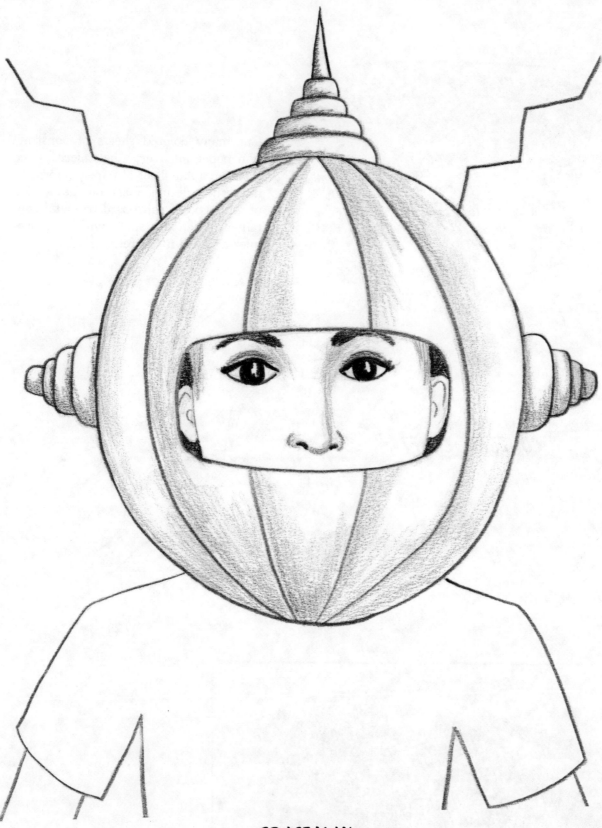

SPACEMAN

Blow up a large round balloon and cover with at least five or six layers of papier mâché. When dry, cut out a large center area and an area in the bottom large enough to accommodate a youngster's head. To the outside add appendages as illustrated, or others that youngsters desire.

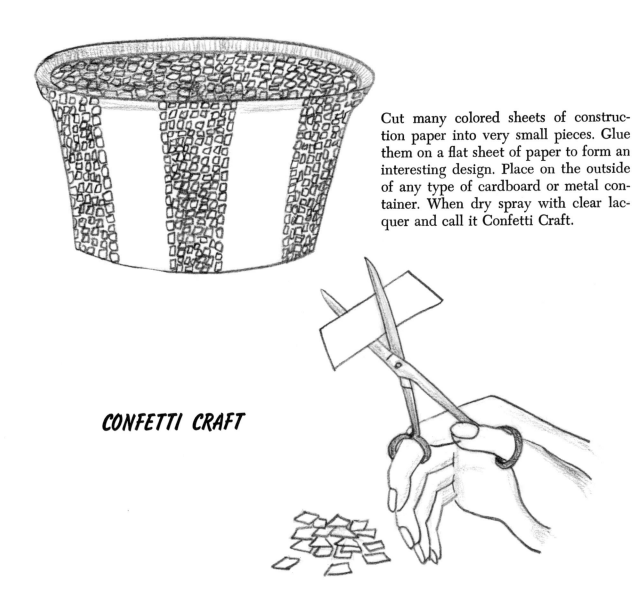

Cut many colored sheets of construction paper into very small pieces. Glue them on a flat sheet of paper to form an interesting design. Place on the outside of any type of cardboard or metal container. When dry spray with clear lacquer and call it Confetti Craft.

CONFETTI CRAFT

PAPIER MÂCHÉ BOWL

Select an attractive bowl or dish that has a top wider than any other part of the dish or bowl. Lubricate the outside surface with vaseline and paste narrow strips of newspaper on this surface. All pieces should overlap. Five or six layers are needed for strength.

Permit to dry and remove from bowl. Trim top and paint with tempera paints. Add a folded strip of paper over the top edge as a finishing step.

TABBY AND TOMMY

Fold a sheet of construction paper in half and cut out
the shape of the legs of your favorite pet. Spread apart
as illustrated and from another sheet of construction
paper, cut out the silhouette of the face. Glue on ears
and other appendages as necessary. Paint eyes, nose and
add whiskers, using pipe cleaners. Attach head to body
and add an appropriate design using construction paper
or colored yarn.

56

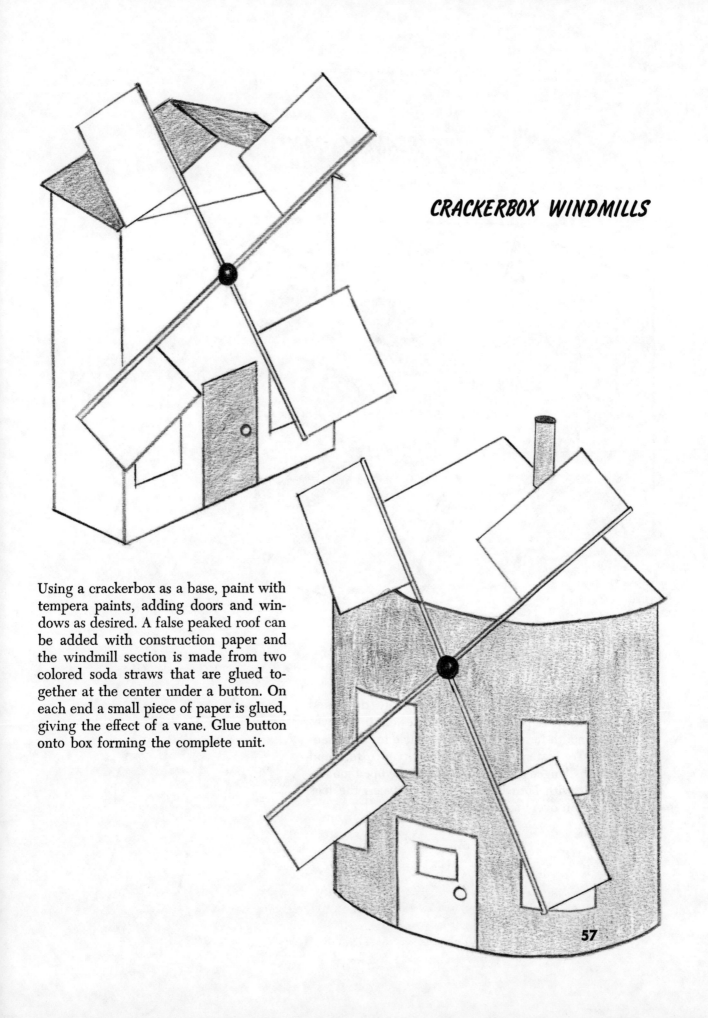

CRACKERBOX WINDMILLS

Using a crackerbox as a base, paint with tempera paints, adding doors and windows as desired. A false peaked roof can be added with construction paper and the windmill section is made from two colored soda straws that are glued together at the center under a button. On each end a small piece of paper is glued, giving the effect of a vane. Glue button onto box forming the complete unit.

57

BEANBAG GAME

A large cardboard box appropriately decorated with tempera paints and with holes cut in for eyes and mouth form the basic receptacle for the beanbag. Youngsters stand off ten or twelve feet and are challenged to toss the bag into the open mouth. Try it with both hands. Try it between the legs and try it over the shoulder.

PINWHEEL

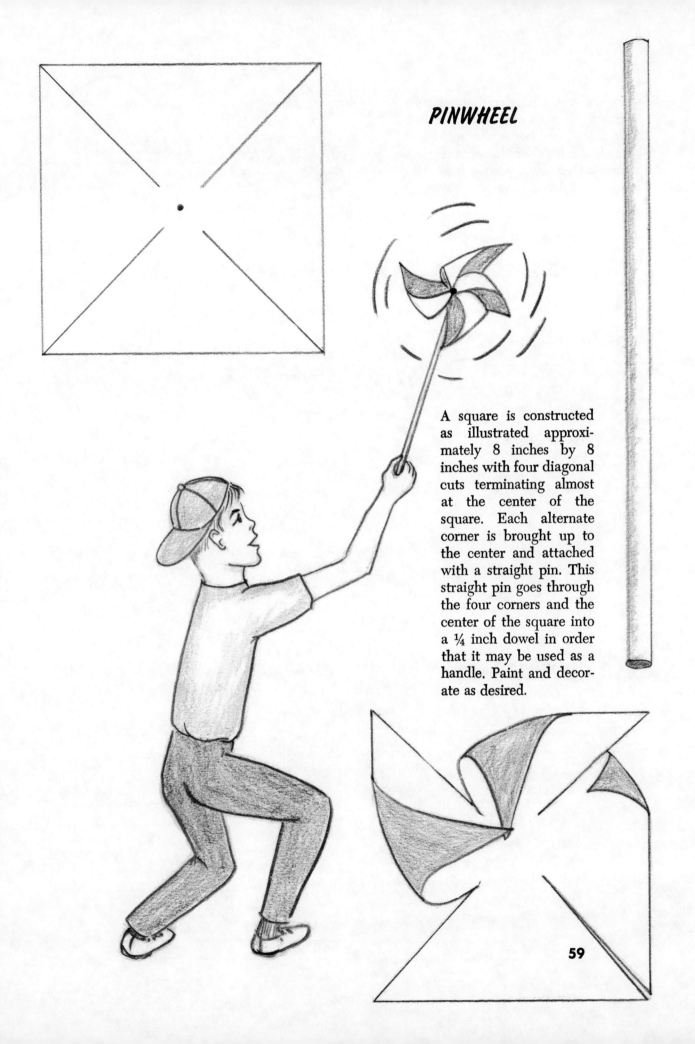

A square is constructed as illustrated approximately 8 inches by 8 inches with four diagonal cuts terminating almost at the center of the square. Each alternate corner is brought up to the center and attached with a straight pin. This straight pin goes through the four corners and the center of the square into a ¼ inch dowel in order that it may be used as a handle. Paint and decorate as desired.

59

Mix fine sand with glue that has been thinned out with water. Pour mixture into a Jello mold or similar mold that has been liberally lubricated with vaseline. Let dry. Remove from container and decorate as you desire.

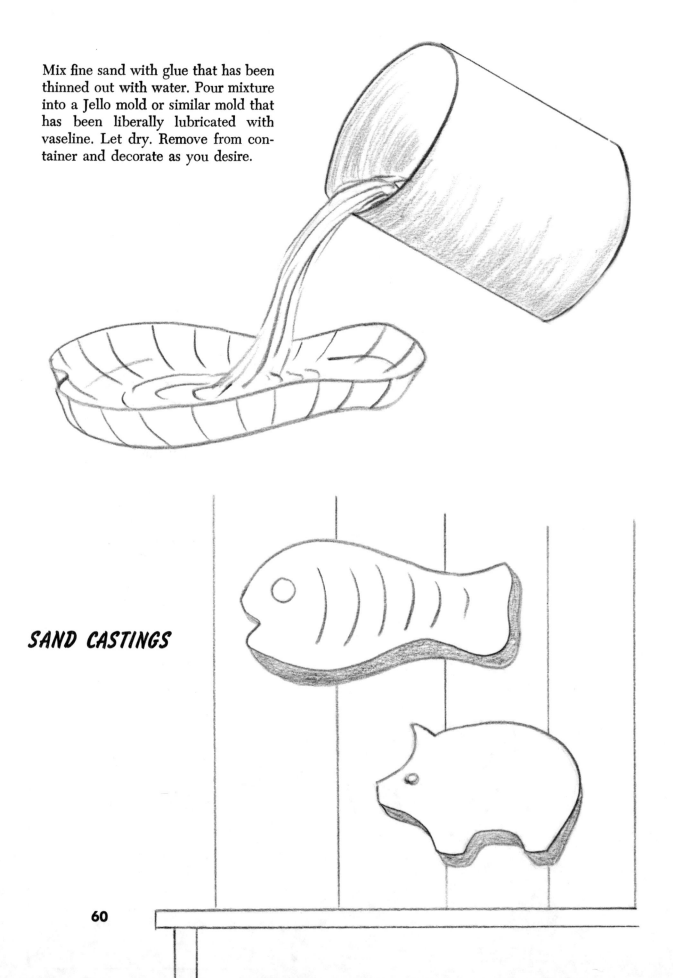

SAND CASTINGS

60

SHELL CHIMES

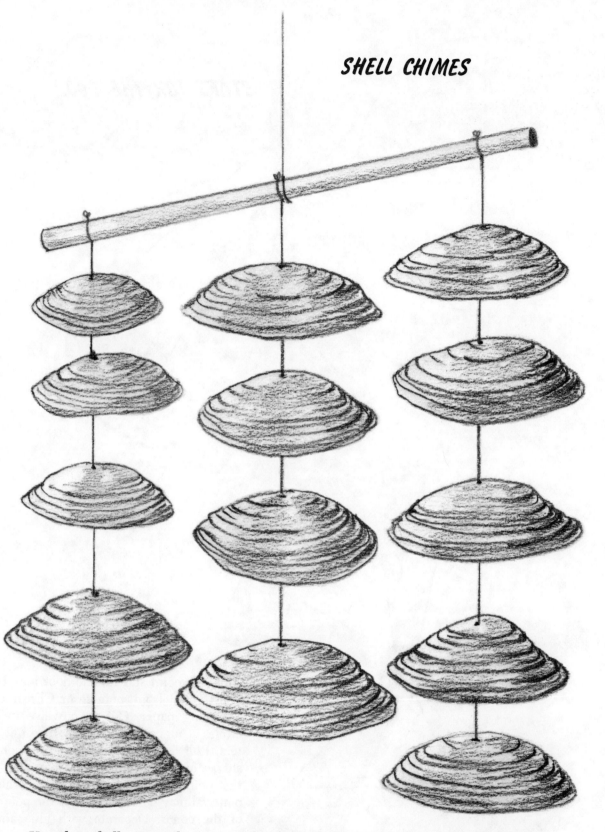

Use clam shells. Turn the upper side of the shell in a downward position. Use a small drill for boring a hole in the apex of the shell. Decorate as much as desired for the completed shells. Insert a string into the hole of each shell and tie a knot into the underside to keep shell from sliding down string. Attach to stick and suspend.

61

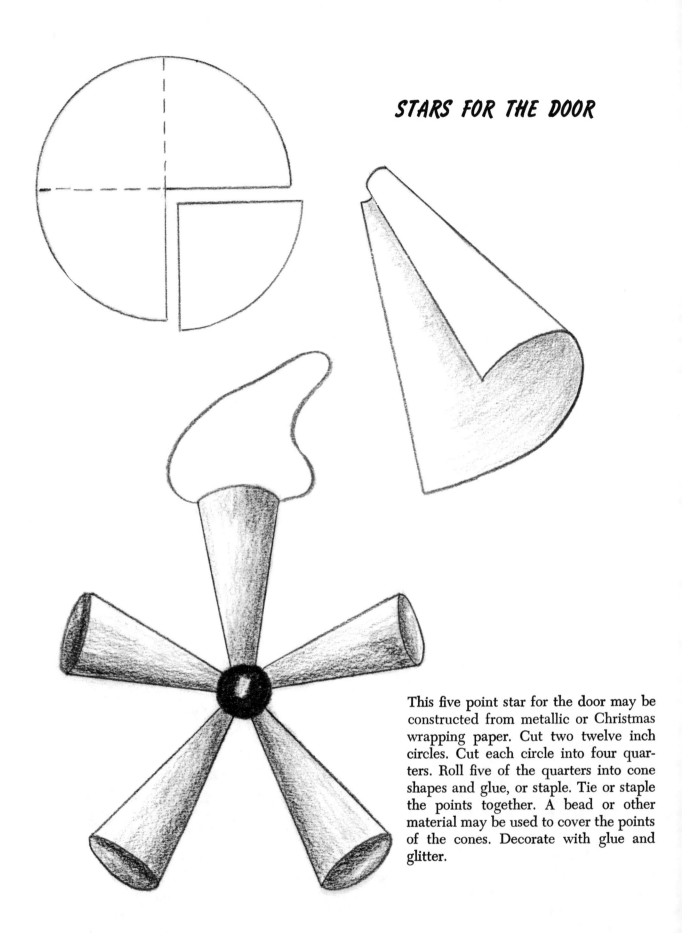

This five point star for the door may be constructed from metallic or Christmas wrapping paper. Cut two twelve inch circles. Cut each circle into four quarters. Roll five of the quarters into cone shapes and glue, or staple. Tie or staple the points together. A bead or other material may be used to cover the points of the cones. Decorate with glue and glitter.

62

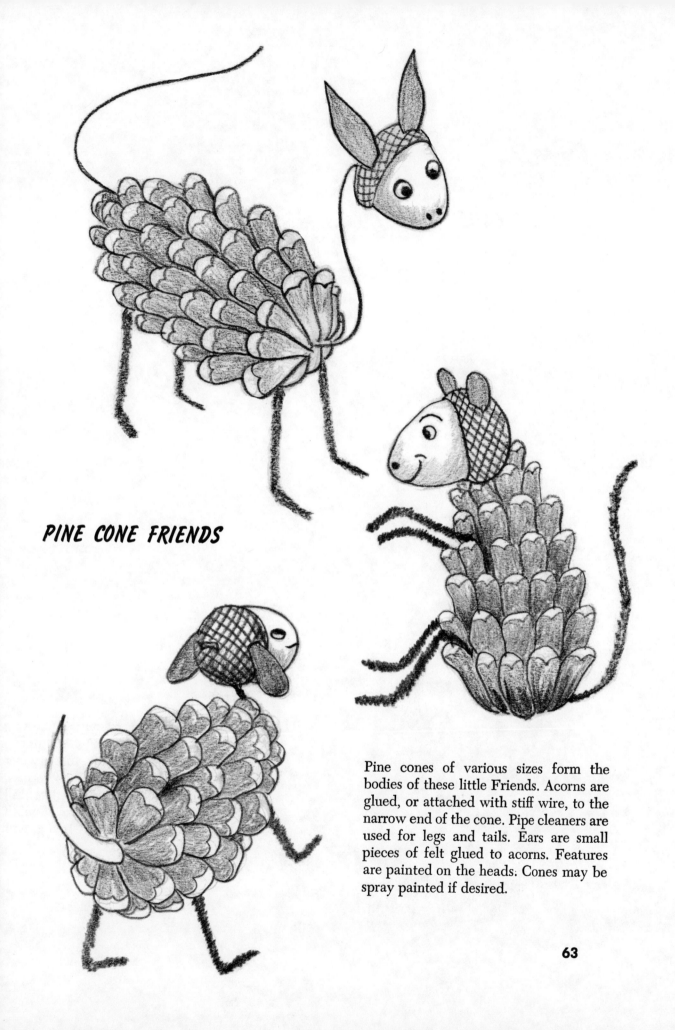

PINE CONE FRIENDS

Pine cones of various sizes form the bodies of these little Friends. Acorns are glued, or attached with stiff wire, to the narrow end of the cone. Pipe cleaners are used for legs and tails. Ears are small pieces of felt glued to acorns. Features are painted on the heads. Cones may be spray painted if desired.

SCENIC OCEANS

Use a mustard jar or any interesting shaped jar with a screw on cap. Fill cap with plasticine. Create underwater scene by inserting interesting figurines, plastic fronds, leaves, and the like. Fill jar with water, add teaspoon of moth flakes. Screw top on tightly. Invert, add felt to bottom.

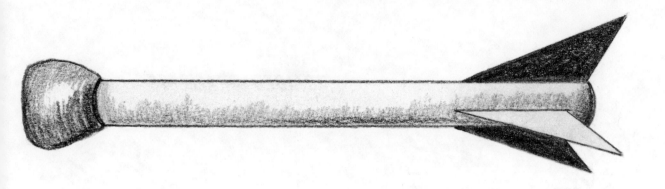

DART GAME

Paint entire cardboard box with a wash coat of water color. Cut several round holes of various sizes in front portion of box. Trim edges of holes with a contrasting color and paint point numbers under holes as indicated in drawing.

Make the dart from ¼″ dowel. On one end use a knife to cut three equidistant slots. Cut three pieces of stiff cardboard as fins. Glue in slots. On other end glue on rubber chair tip.

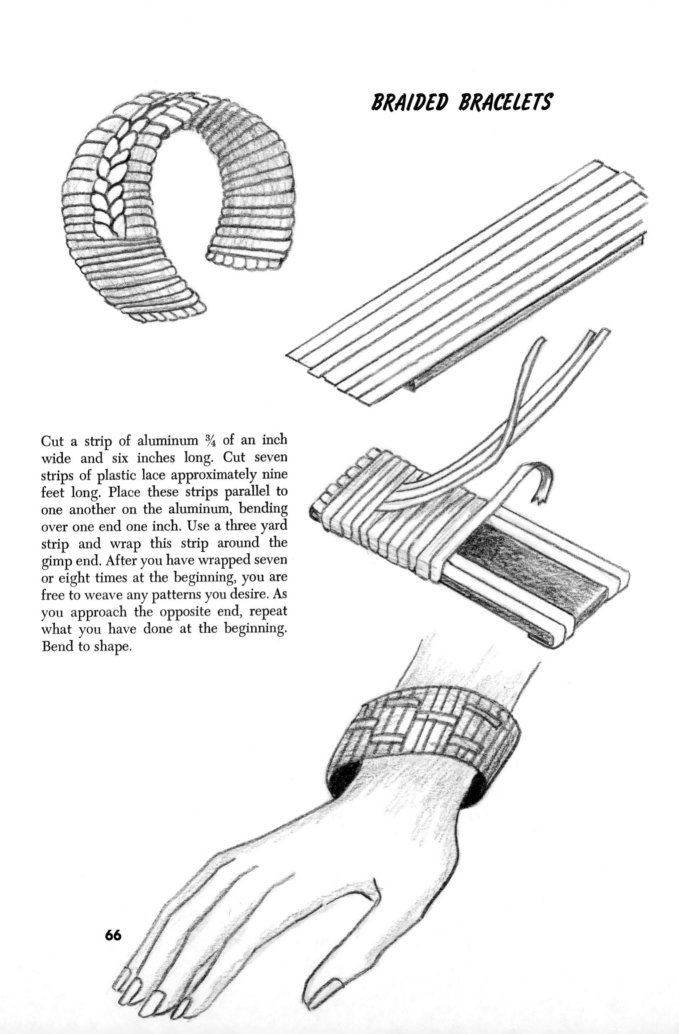

Cut a strip of aluminum ¾ of an inch wide and six inches long. Cut seven strips of plastic lace approximately nine feet long. Place these strips parallel to one another on the aluminum, bending over one end one inch. Use a three yard strip and wrap this strip around the gimp end. After you have wrapped seven or eight times at the beginning, you are free to weave any patterns you desire. As you approach the opposite end, repeat what you have done at the beginning. Bend to shape.

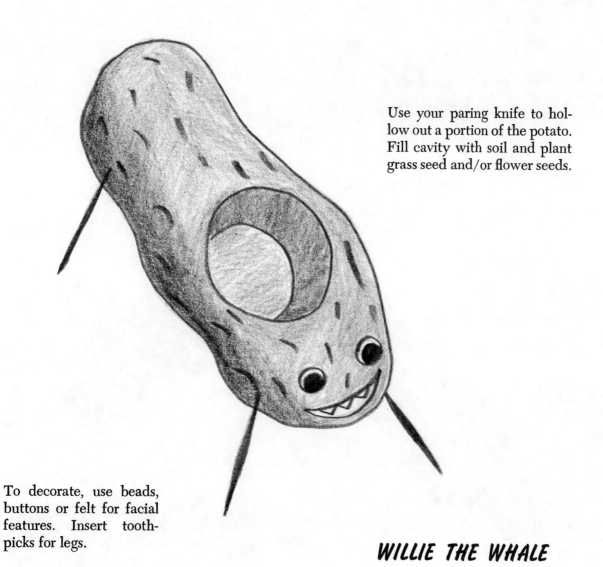

Use your paring knife to hollow out a portion of the potato. Fill cavity with soil and plant grass seed and/or flower seeds.

To decorate, use beads, buttons or felt for facial features. Insert toothpicks for legs.

WILLIE THE WHALE

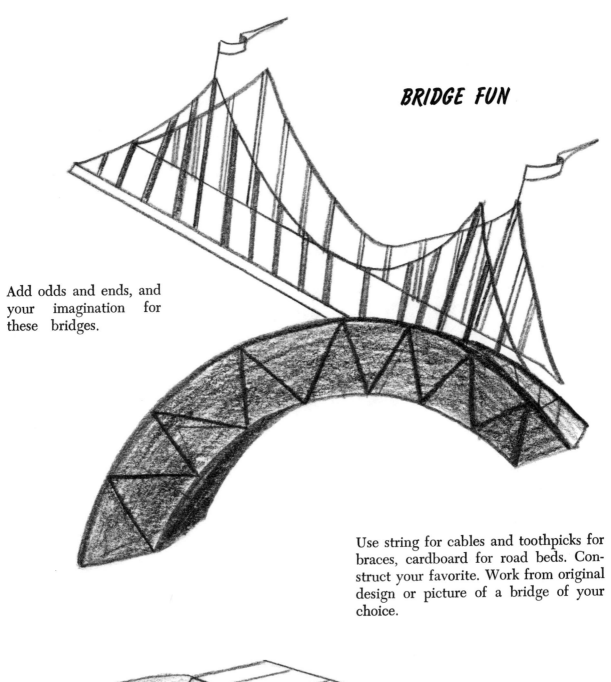

BRIDGE FUN

Add odds and ends, and your imagination for these bridges.

Use string for cables and toothpicks for braces, cardboard for road beds. Construct your favorite. Work from original design or picture of a bridge of your choice.

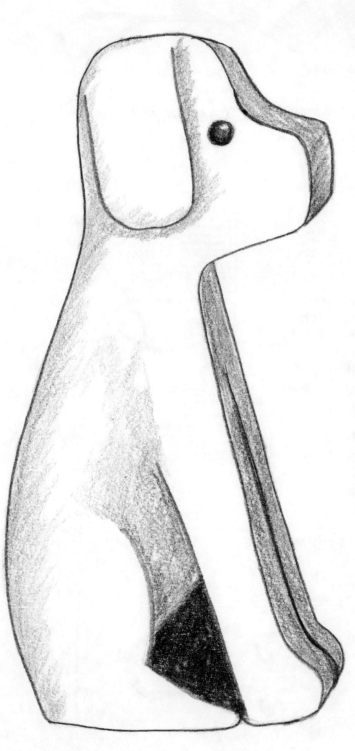

Mix ½ verniculite with ½ plaster of Paris. Slowly add this mixture to water. (See directions on mixing plaster of Paris.) Fill milk carton with mixture. Permit to set. Tear off milk carton. Carve with knife or large wood screw and smooth with sandpaper. Paint with tempera paints. Spray with clear lacquer. Attach felt to bottom of carved object.

PLASTER OF PARIS CARVINGS

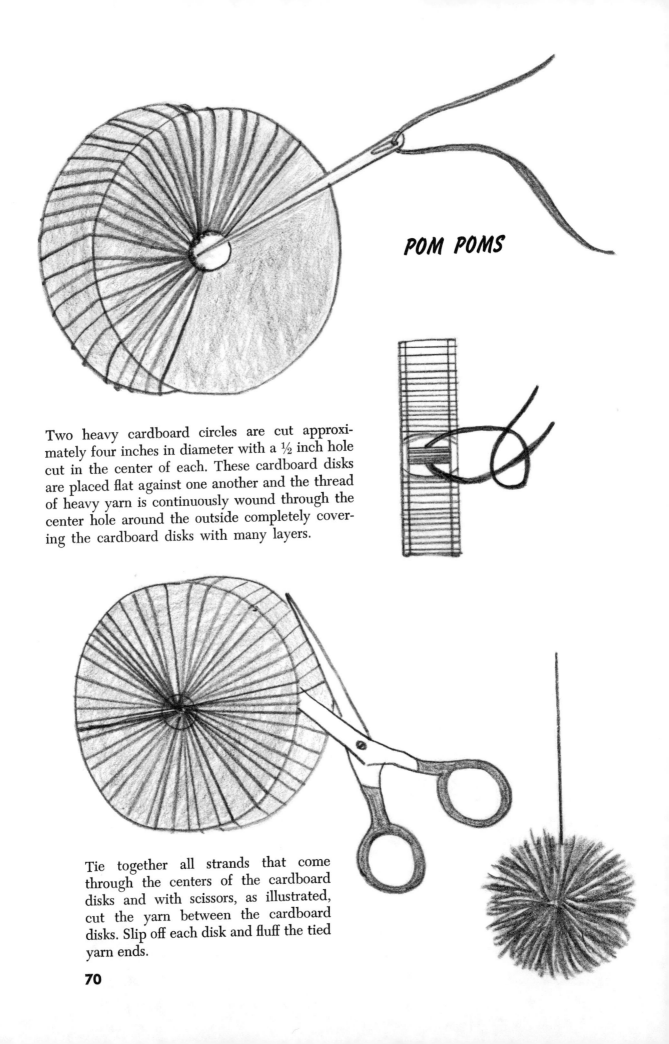

POM POMS

Two heavy cardboard circles are cut approximately four inches in diameter with a ½ inch hole cut in the center of each. These cardboard disks are placed flat against one another and the thread of heavy yarn is continuously wound through the center hole around the outside completely covering the cardboard disks with many layers.

Tie together all strands that come through the centers of the cardboard disks and with scissors, as illustrated, cut the yarn between the cardboard disks. Slip off each disk and fluff the tied yarn ends.

TODAY AND TOMORROW

These delightful creatures are created by using a large cork and adding features from construction paper. The porcupine has large headed straight pins added to simulate quills. Small pieces of felt are attached to base as legs.

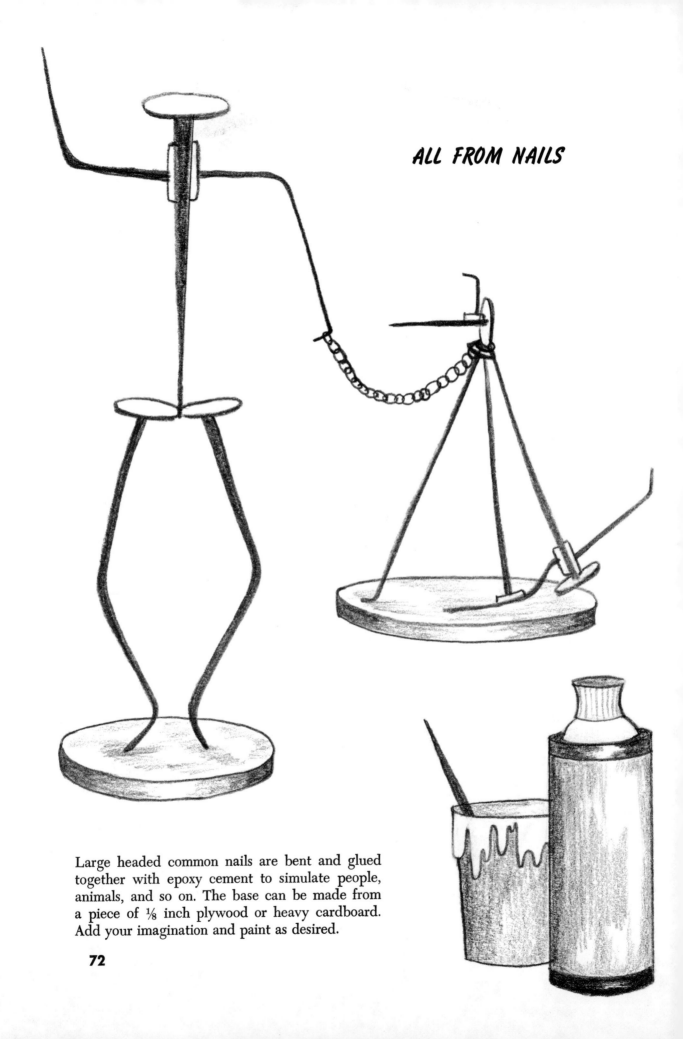

Large headed common nails are bent and glued together with epoxy cement to simulate people, animals, and so on. The base can be made from a piece of ⅛ inch plywood or heavy cardboard. Add your imagination and paint as desired.

ALL FROM STICKS

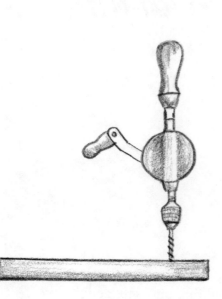

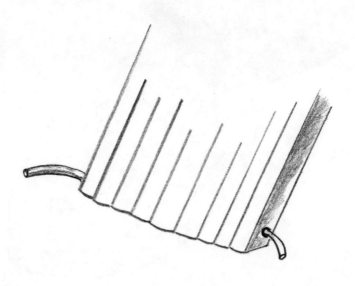

Cut a series of sticks approximately ¼ x ¼ by four inches long. Through each end drill a small hole, using a ¹⁄₁₆ inch twist bit and a hand drill. As illustrated, thread through a piece of wire, bending the ends over the end sticks to hold in place. Add a dab of glue to each end. Paint and decorate as desired.

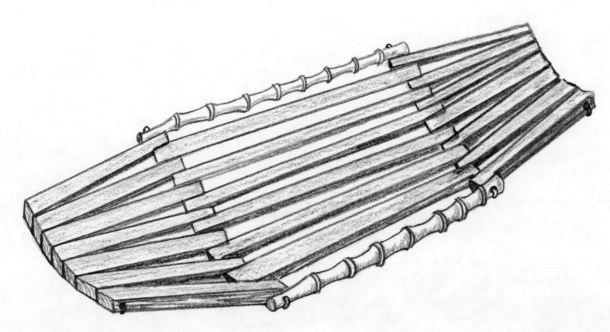

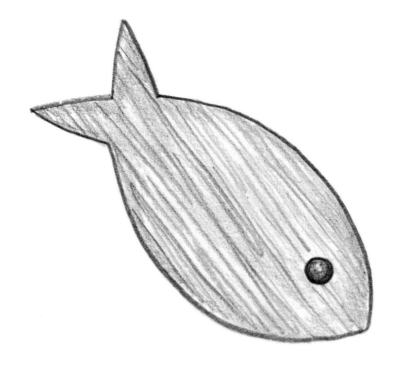

FLAT PINS

These delightful pins are designed to meet your individual needs. They are cut from a piece of 1/8 or 3/16 inch soft pine and sanded smooth. Features are added and the unit can be painted or stained. Finish up with a clear coat of lacquer or shellac. Glue a pin back to the reverse side.

FROM THE SEA

These mobiles are designed using construction paper and/or white drawing paper with the silhouette cut with scissors. Marking pens of various colors are used to form the basic designs. Sewing thread is glued to the center of gravity of each unit and supported as illustrated.

75

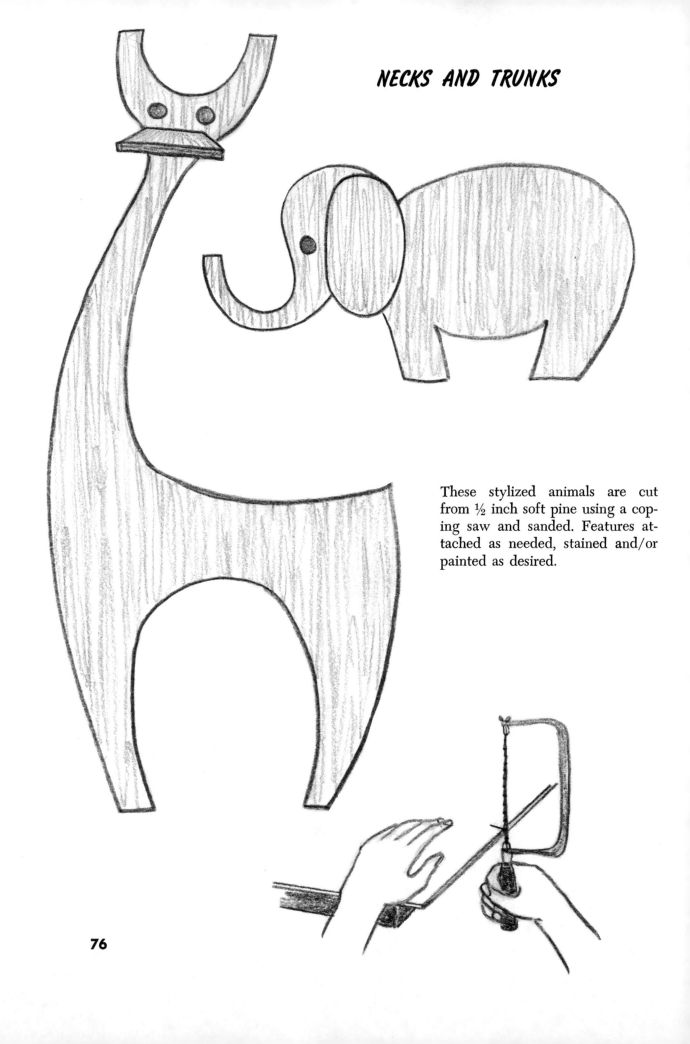

These stylized animals are cut from ½ inch soft pine using a coping saw and sanded. Features attached as needed, stained and/or painted as desired.

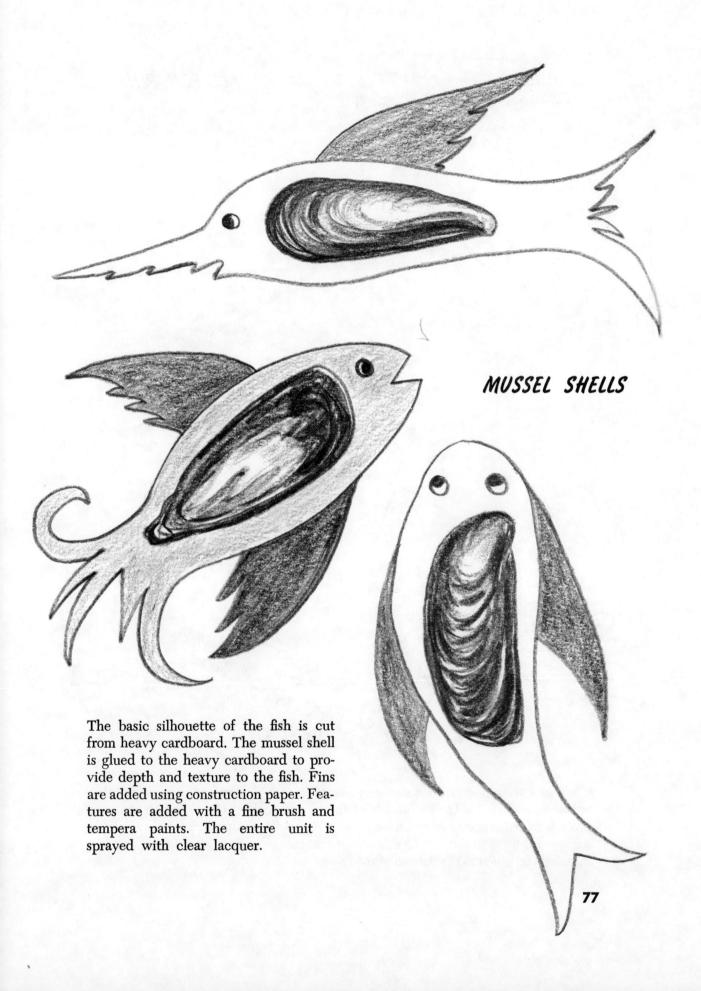

MUSSEL SHELLS

The basic silhouette of the fish is cut from heavy cardboard. The mussel shell is glued to the heavy cardboard to provide depth and texture to the fish. Fins are added using construction paper. Features are added with a fine brush and tempera paints. The entire unit is sprayed with clear lacquer.

77

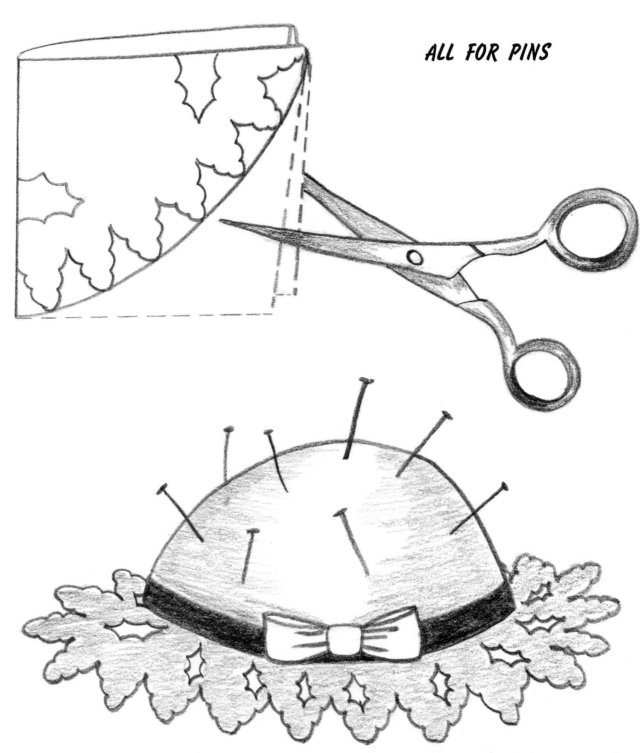

A half of a styrofoam ball forms the crown of the cushion and an attractive ribbon and bow are fastened to the flat side of the crown. A sheet of colored construction paper is folded twice as illustrated and with a pencil a design is created as desired. Scissors are used to cut the four layers simultaneously. The construction paper is unfolded and glued to the bottom of the crown.

SAILING KNICK KNACK

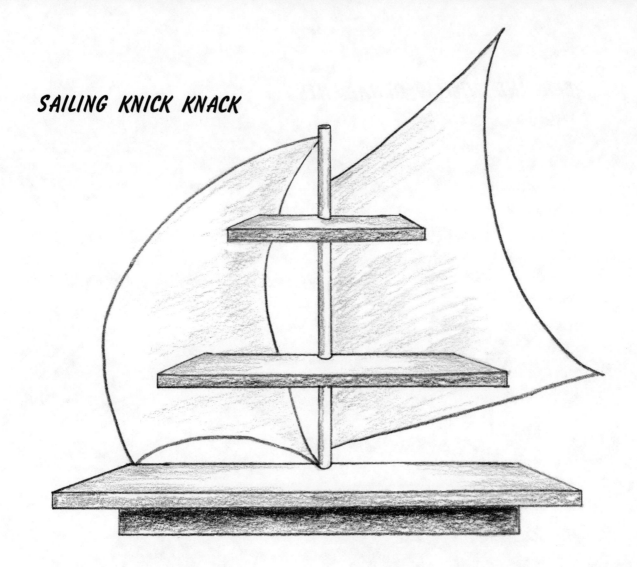

The hull of this hanging shelf is made from a piece of ½ inch pine, three inches wide and approximately eighteen inches long. As illustrated, a ¼ inch dowel provides the main mast to which two other shelves are attached. The sails are cut from flat stiff white cardboard and merely glued at the points of contact. These sails remain flat against the shelves and against the wall to which the unit is attached. Stain and/or paint as desired.

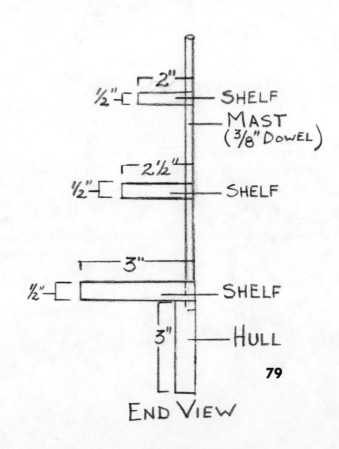

END VIEW

REED AND WILLOW ORNAMENTS

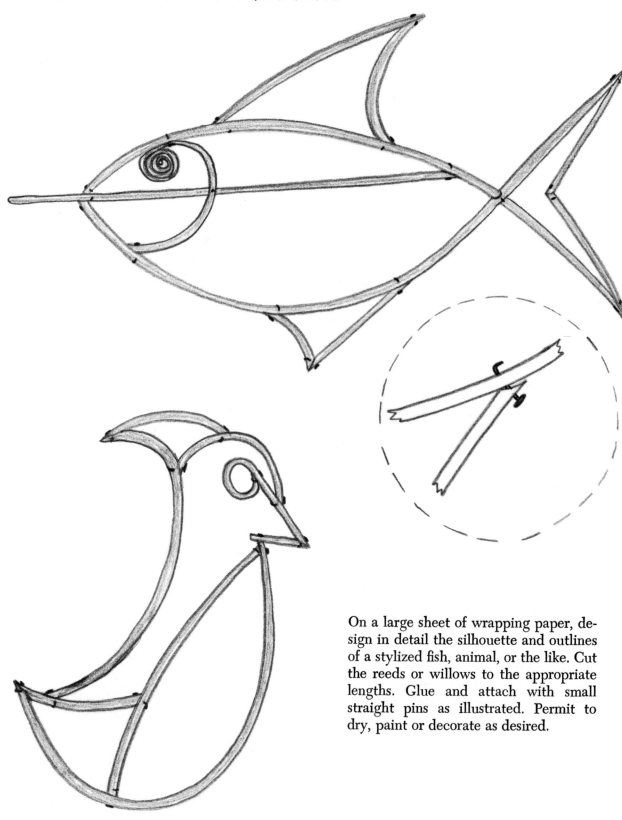

On a large sheet of wrapping paper, design in detail the silhouette and outlines of a stylized fish, animal, or the like. Cut the reeds or willows to the appropriate lengths. Glue and attach with small straight pins as illustrated. Permit to dry, paint or decorate as desired.

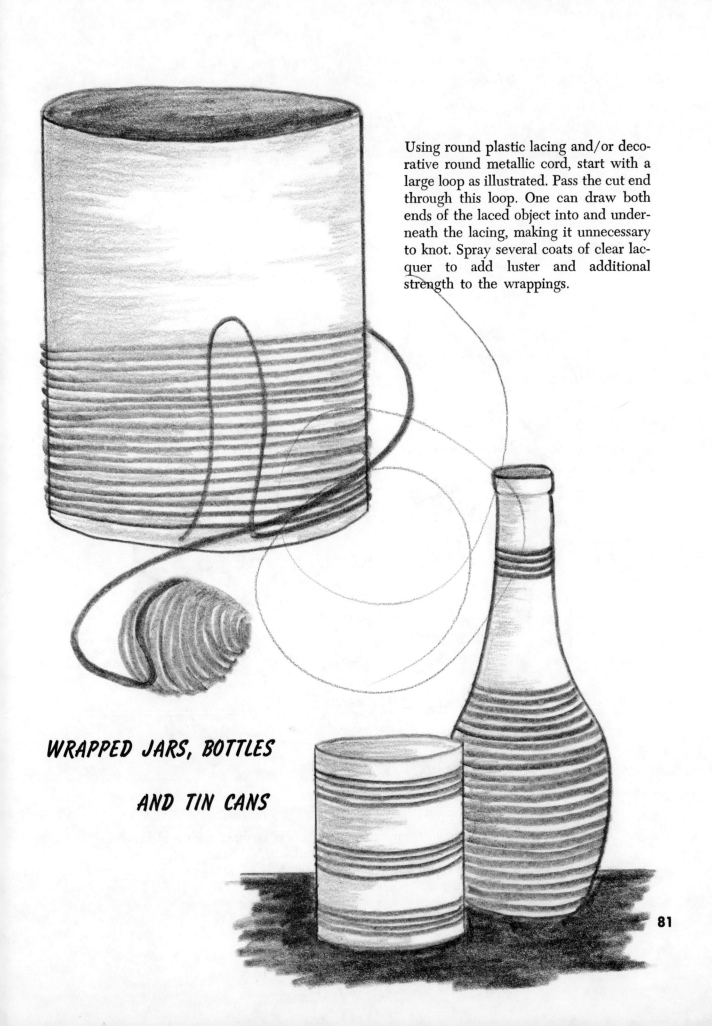

Using round plastic lacing and/or decorative round metallic cord, start with a large loop as illustrated. Pass the cut end through this loop. One can draw both ends of the laced object into and underneath the lacing, making it unnecessary to knot. Spray several coats of clear lacquer to add luster and additional strength to the wrappings.

WRAPPED JARS, BOTTLES

AND TIN CANS

TRINKET BOX

These trinket boxes are made from square and round sardine, tuna and salmon cans. After being very well washed, they are painted with oil paints and decorated as desired with marbles of equal size glued on to the bottom as legs.

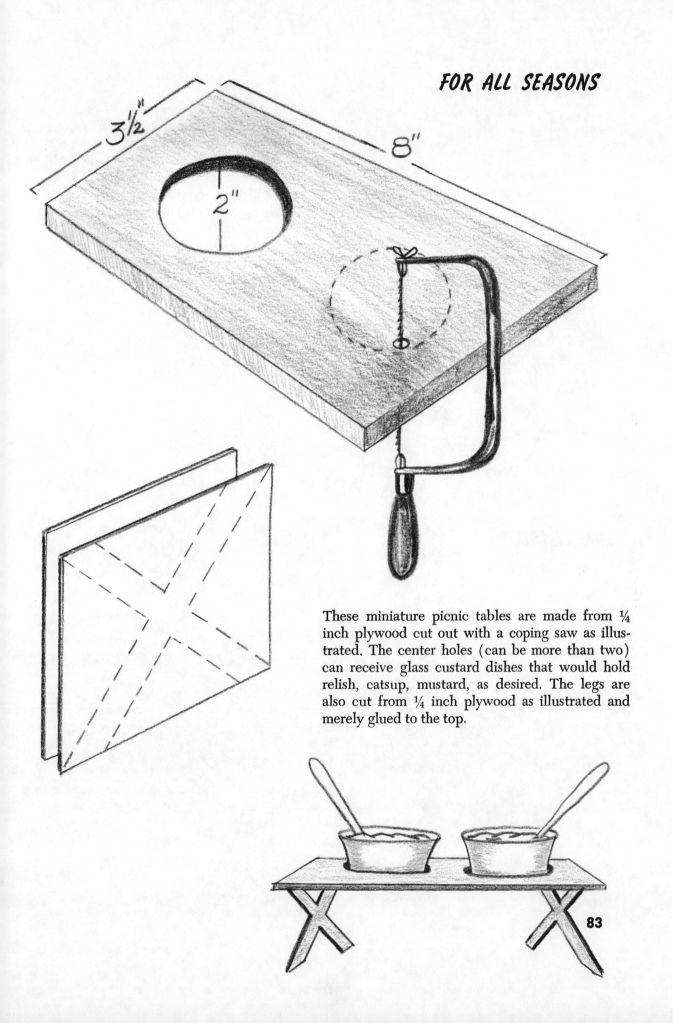

3½"

8"

2"

These miniature picnic tables are made from ¼ inch plywood cut out with a coping saw as illustrated. The center holes (can be more than two) can receive glass custard dishes that would hold relish, catsup, mustard, as desired. The legs are also cut from ¼ inch plywood as illustrated and merely glued to the top.

83

Virtually any size tin cans are used for this purpose. The holder is constructed from a one inch dowel that has been cut to four inches in length. About one inch from the top of this dowel a ⅜ inch hole is drilled to receive a ⅜ inch dowel. Each can has two holes punched one inch apart approximately half way down to receive soft wire. This wire is threaded through each can and is carefully wrapped and passed through a ¼ inch hole that has been drilled in the handle. These cans are painted and decorated as desired.

COKE CADDY

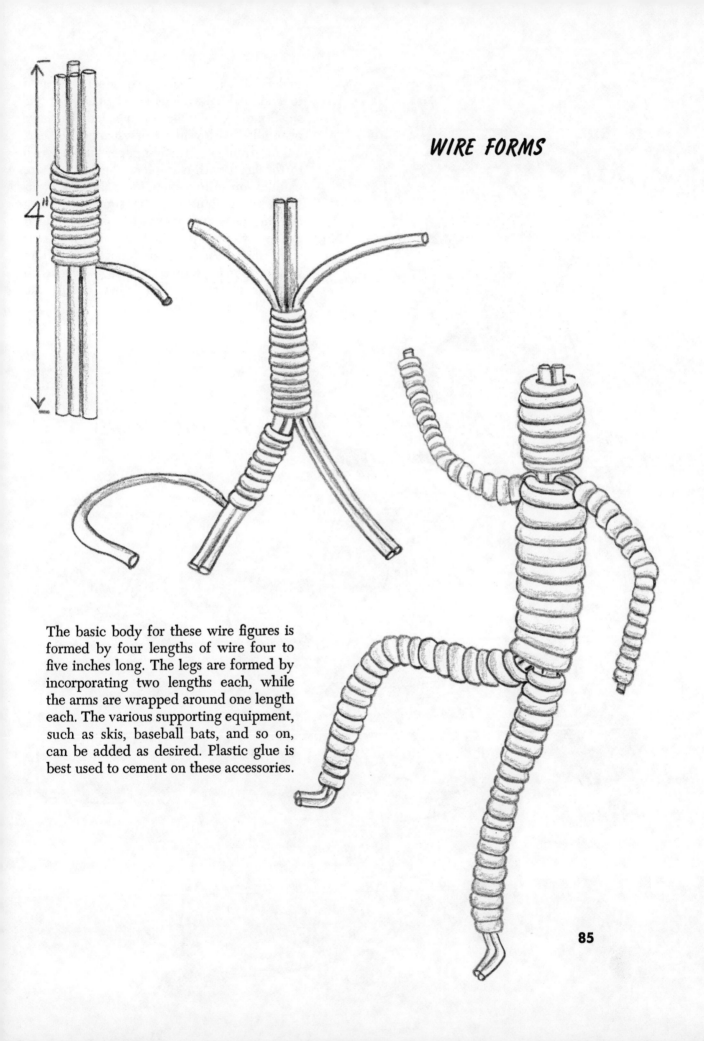

4"

The basic body for these wire figures is formed by four lengths of wire four to five inches long. The legs are formed by incorporating two lengths each, while the arms are wrapped around one length each. The various supporting equipment, such as skis, baseball bats, and so on, can be added as desired. Plastic glue is best used to cement on these accessories.

85

Paper bags in all sizes are effectively used to create these various sized mice. For the small mouse, two bags are needed that have been filled with wads of newspaper. The ears are cut from construction paper and fastened to the head with a stapler. The features are painted on using tempera paints. Various types of clothing can be simulated using marking pens and paints. The feet are glued to the bottom of the filled bag. For the larger sized mice, the ears are constructed from small paper bags that have been filled with wadded newspaper. All other details are similar to the small mouse.

THE MICE FAMILY

PINE CONE TREE

A heavy piece of cardboard or ¼ inch plywood forms the back of this tree. It is sprayed gold or silver and down the center is a ¼ inch dowel rod glued as illustrated. This dowel rod is glued directly to the cone shaped backing. A series of pine cones, working from the bottom to the top in various lengths and sizes are glued both to the dowel and the backing. The final cone is glued directly to the end of the dowel. Using a small brush, the ends of these cones can be highlighted with gold or silver paint as desired.

A heavy strip of cardboard is cut four inches wide and thirty-six inches long. The ends are stapled together forming a ring about twelve inches in diameter. A thin piece of string is passed through the center and a large knot is tied to support the ring. From each side of the center of the ring strings are attached that support styrofoam balls or circles cut from construction paper. Other features are added as illustrated. Hats, bows, and so on, are designed and added as desired.

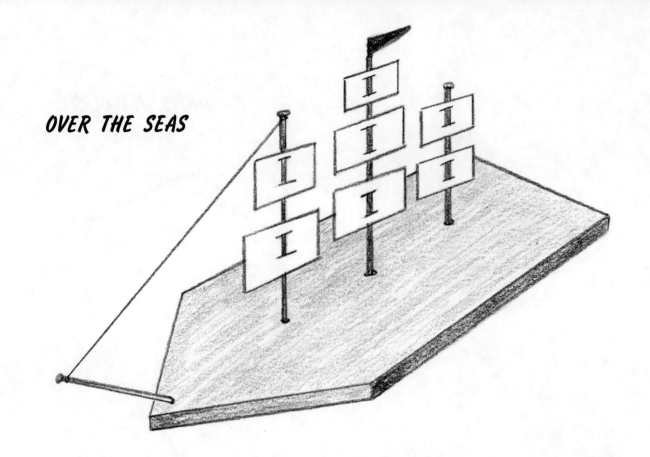

OVER THE SEAS

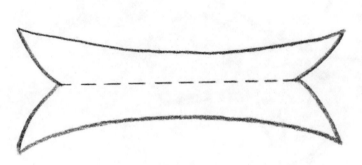

Flat square riggers are made from small pieces of pine cut at an angle to form the bow. The masts are made from large finishing nails. The sails are designed as desired with small slits as illustrated, to receive the masts. Thin string can be used to simulate the rigging. Canoes and double ended boats are constructed from construction paper that has been folded down the center and cut with scissors as illustrated. The ends are held together with tape. The thwarts and seats are added as illustrated.

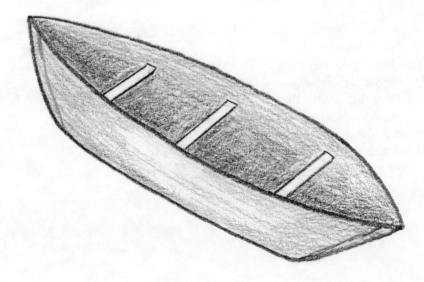

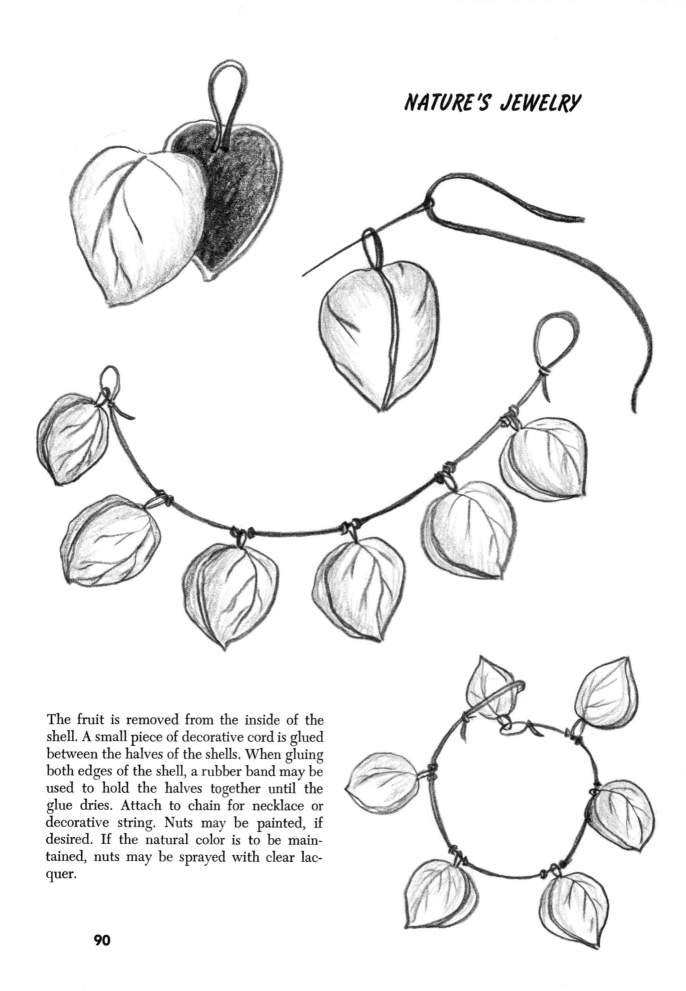

The fruit is removed from the inside of the shell. A small piece of decorative cord is glued between the halves of the shells. When gluing both edges of the shell, a rubber band may be used to hold the halves together until the glue dries. Attach to chain for necklace or decorative string. Nuts may be painted, if desired. If the natural color is to be maintained, nuts may be sprayed with clear lacquer.

90

LUNCH TIME

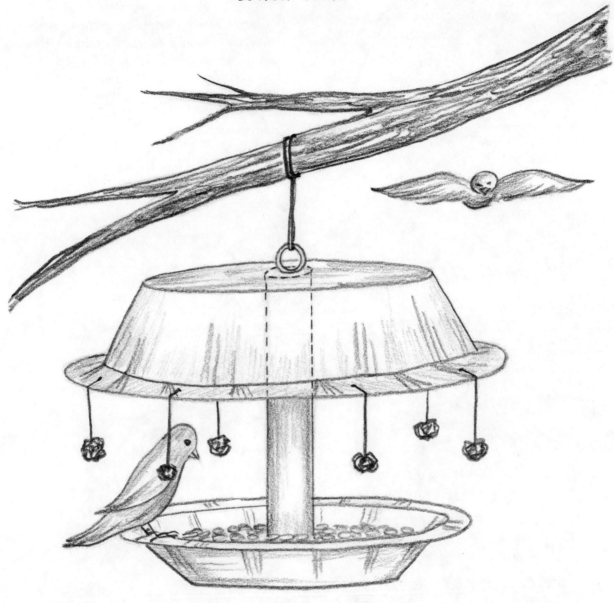

Separated by a one inch dowel six inches in length, are two aluminum pie tins. The smaller bottom tin is fastened to the dowel by a small large headed nail that is driven through the center of the bottom pan and into the dowel. The upper pan is fastened with a small screw eye to the dowel. The screw eye provides a means of hanging. Small holes are punched in the rim of the upper pan and strings inserted for hanging of suet. Pans may be painted, if desired.

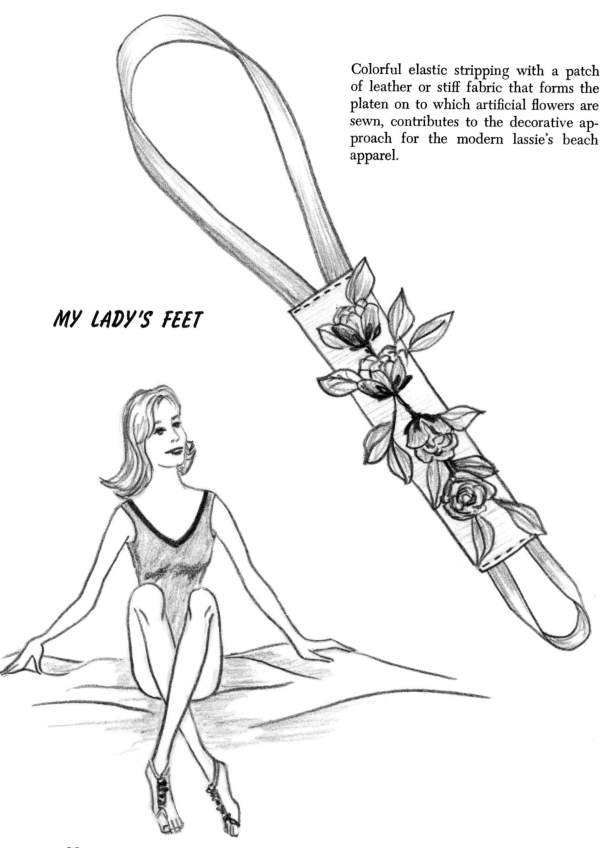

Colorful elastic stripping with a patch of leather or stiff fabric that forms the platen on to which artificial flowers are sewn, contributes to the decorative approach for the modern lassie's beach apparel.

MY LADY'S FEET

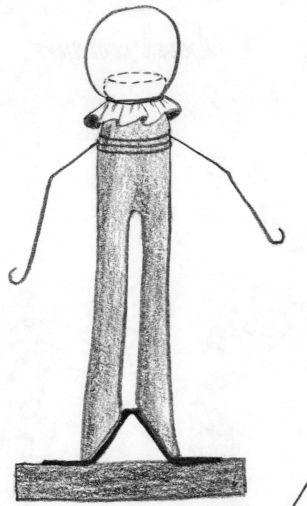

CLOTHESPIN PEOPLE

To enlarge the head of the clothespin, a small circular piece of crepe paper is stuffed with cotton and carefully stretched over the head of the pin and tied at the neck with string. Features are painted on the crepe paper and/or sequins glued on as desired.

Hair is from yarn and styled as desired. Clothing is from construction paper or remnants of materials. Arms are from pipe cleaners with small holes drilled into the clothespins to receive the ends of the pipe cleaners. Small pieces of cardboard are glued to tapered feet and fastened to a base.

93

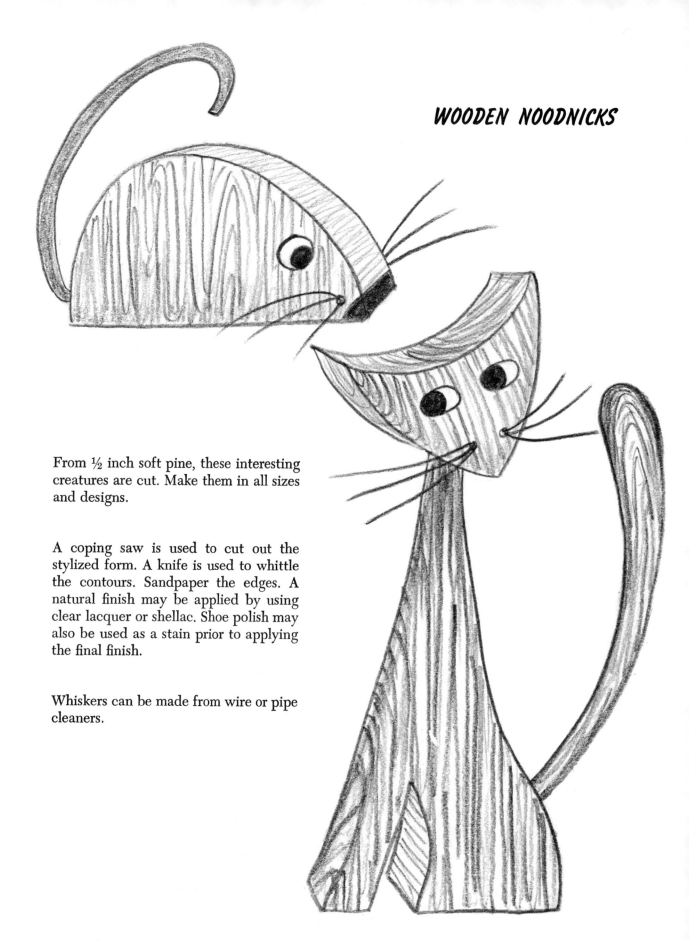

WOODEN NOODNICKS

From ½ inch soft pine, these interesting creatures are cut. Make them in all sizes and designs.

A coping saw is used to cut out the stylized form. A knife is used to whittle the contours. Sandpaper the edges. A natural finish may be applied by using clear lacquer or shellac. Shoe polish may also be used as a stain prior to applying the final finish.

Whiskers can be made from wire or pipe cleaners.

TO THE RACES

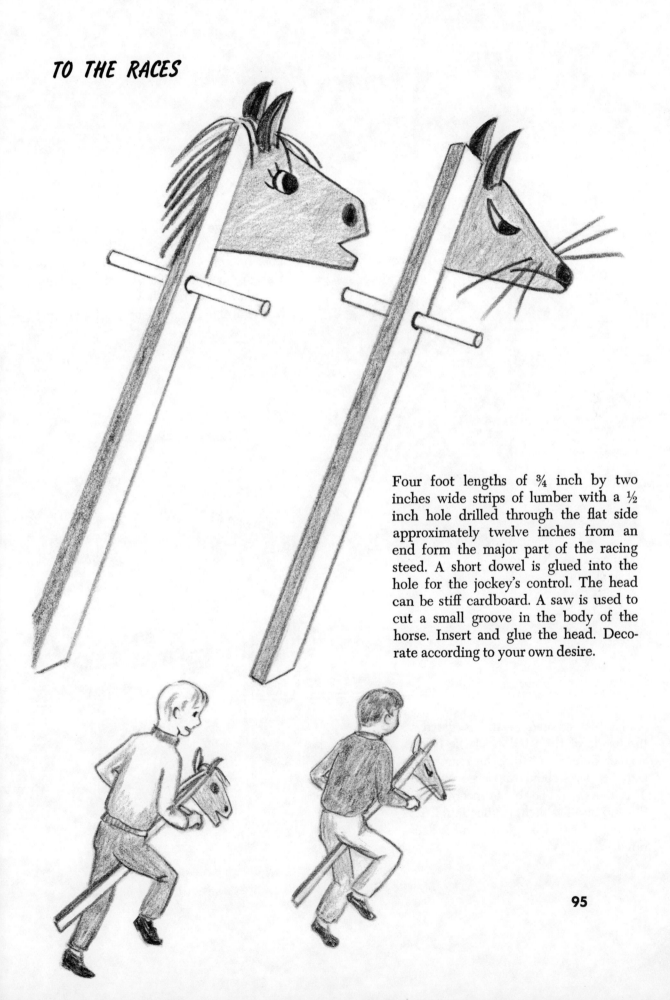

Four foot lengths of ¾ inch by two inches wide strips of lumber with a ½ inch hole drilled through the flat side approximately twelve inches from an end form the major part of the racing steed. A short dowel is glued into the hole for the jockey's control. The head can be stiff cardboard. A saw is used to cut a small groove in the body of the horse. Insert and glue the head. Decorate according to your own desire.

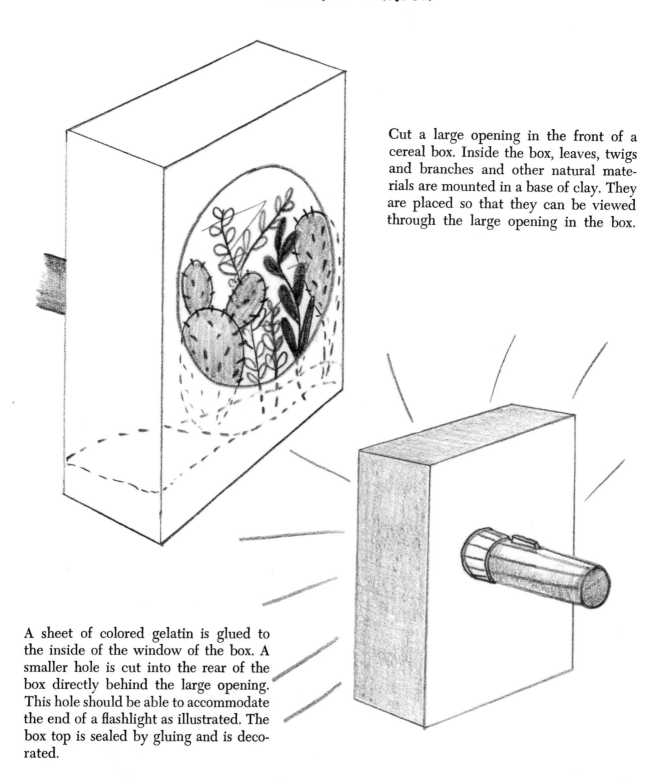

Cut a large opening in the front of a cereal box. Inside the box, leaves, twigs and branches and other natural materials are mounted in a base of clay. They are placed so that they can be viewed through the large opening in the box.

A sheet of colored gelatin is glued to the inside of the window of the box. A smaller hole is cut into the rear of the box directly behind the large opening. This hole should be able to accommodate the end of a flashlight as illustrated. The box top is sealed by gluing and is decorated.

PENGUIN ISLAND

Discarded light bulbs that have been painted half black and half white are used to simulate this interesting creature. A yellow golf tee is glued to the contact end of the bulb. Wings are from construction paper and glued to the appropriate positions on the body.

Other addendums are attached to individualize your creation. The body is glued to a cardboard coaster.

97

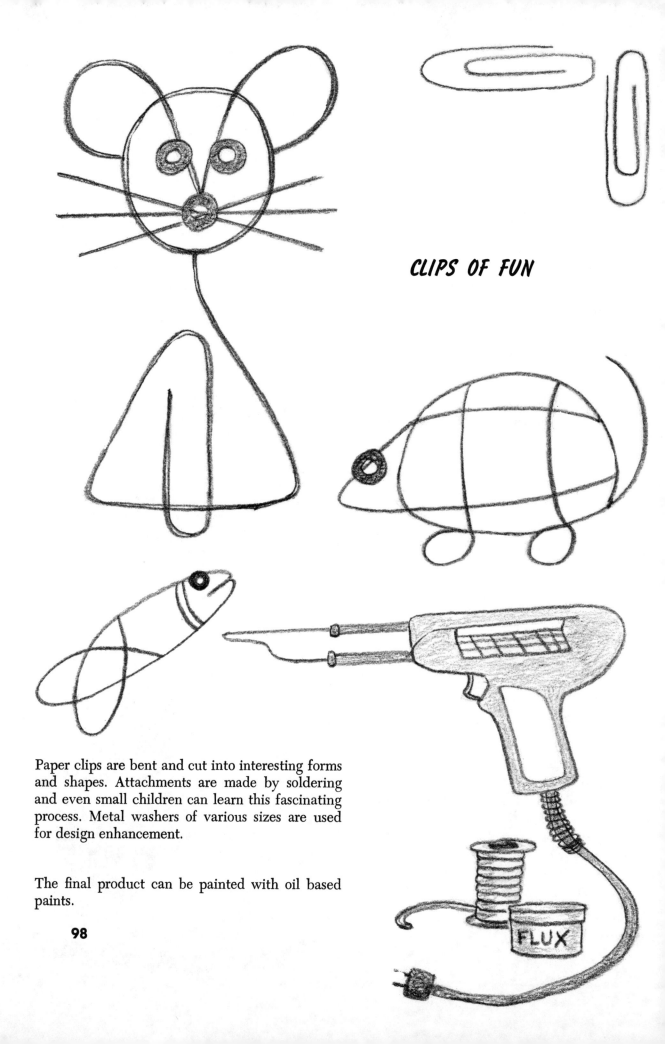

CLIPS OF FUN

Paper clips are bent and cut into interesting forms and shapes. Attachments are made by soldering and even small children can learn this fascinating process. Metal washers of various sizes are used for design enhancement.

The final product can be painted with oil based paints.

98

FLUX

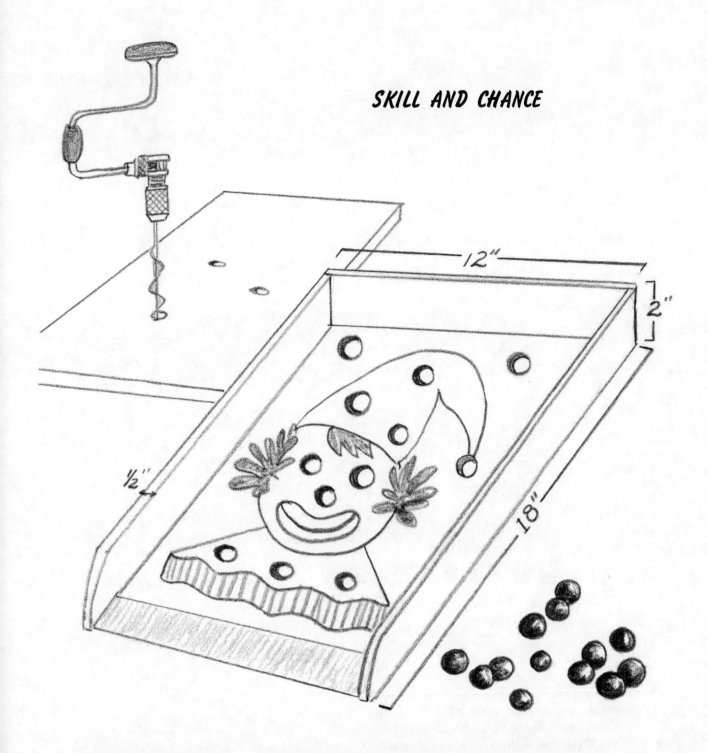

A piece of ¼ inch plywood approximately twelve by eighteen inches is used as the base of this game. The painted design should be applied and holes bored in appropriate places with a ½ inch auger bit. One end of the base is planed to a feather edge. The sides are fastened by using small brads that are driven through the base. Number values may be painted or glued on, if desired.

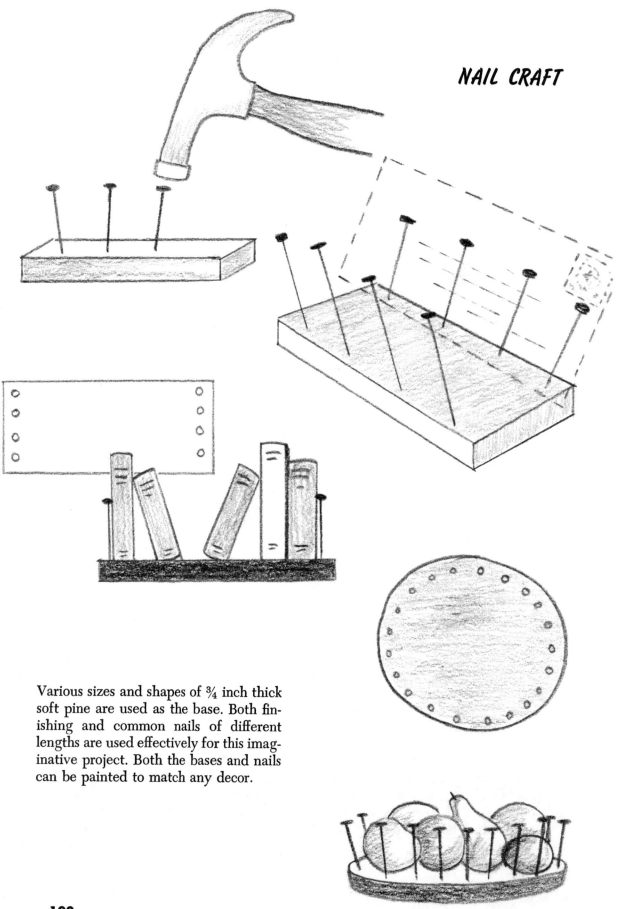

Various sizes and shapes of ¾ inch thick soft pine are used as the base. Both finishing and common nails of different lengths are used effectively for this imaginative project. Both the bases and nails can be painted to match any decor.

PAPER PLATE CRAFT

Gesso is mixed in a glass jar according to directions on container. Keep mixing jar in hot water while working on the project. Coat both sides of three inexpensive quality paper plates with gesso. Press them together. Be certain that the edges are in contact with one another. Place under a heavy weight while drying. Apply additional layers of gesso, carefully smoothing the edges and filling any small holes. When last coat is thoroughly dry, smooth with fine sandpaper. Paint with semigloss enamel paint. With a fine brush and using gold or silver paint, create a desired design. When dry, apply shellac.

FROM OUT OF SPACE

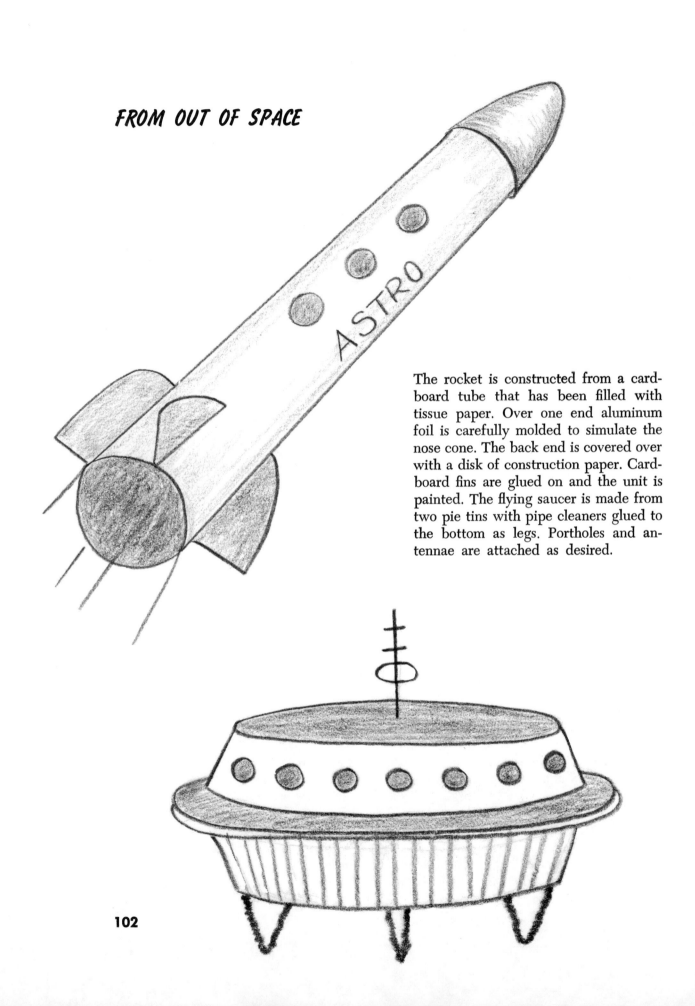

The rocket is constructed from a cardboard tube that has been filled with tissue paper. Over one end aluminum foil is carefully molded to simulate the nose cone. The back end is covered over with a disk of construction paper. Cardboard fins are glued on and the unit is painted. The flying saucer is made from two pie tins with pipe cleaners glued to the bottom as legs. Portholes and antennae are attached as desired.

ODDS AND ENDS BOX

Use a cottage cheese box with large buttons added to simulate wheels and soda straws as wagon tongues. The handle of the pail is made using pipe cleaners. Additional decorations using casine paints will enhance its beauty.

CARVED WOODEN WARE

This project is for the older boys and girls where a workbench and various gouges, mallets and clamps are available. The design is drawn on soft pine and the inside is cut out using a mallet and gouge. Work from the outside towards the center to avoid splitting the edge. When cut to a sufficient depth, a coping saw can be used to cut away the additional materials. Sand smooth.

104

Write your name on a piece of tracing paper. Turn paper over and with carbon paper underneath, trace your name on a small piece of masonite. (Your name will appear on the masonite in reverse order.) Glue string to traced line. Permit to dry. Attach thread spool by gluing to reverse side of masonite. When thoroughly dry, ink on stamp pad and enjoy the results.

MUSICAL HUMMERS

A cardboard tube with one end covered with wax paper that is held in place by a rubber band forms the basic unit. A series of holes that are alternately covered and uncovered by the player's fingers are punched into the tube. Musical sounds are created by holding the open end against one's mouth as you hum into the end. Decorate as desired.

DESK ACCESSORY

This attractive accessory is made from a two quart milk container cut to an appropriate height and covered with decorative Christmas wrappings. Use a base with four ⅛ inch holes. Wire coat hangers bent in the form of U's, and held together by wooden beads that are glued on the wires, will form the decorative railing around the container. Paint as desired.

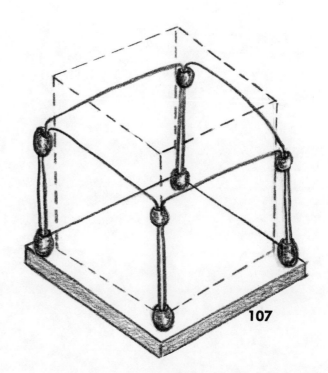

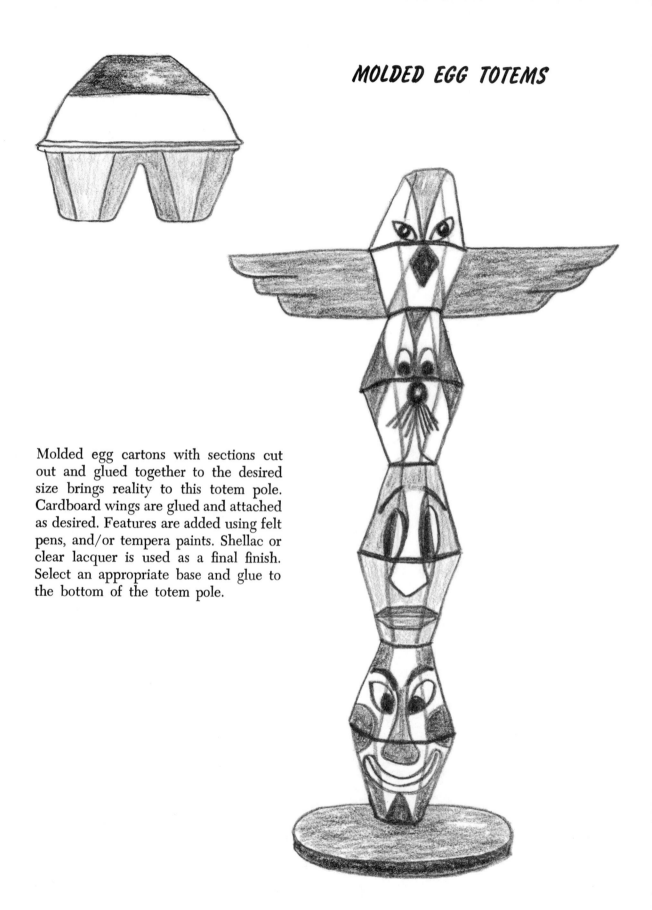

Molded egg cartons with sections cut out and glued together to the desired size brings reality to this totem pole. Cardboard wings are glued and attached as desired. Features are added using felt pens, and/or tempera paints. Shellac or clear lacquer is used as a final finish. Select an appropriate base and glue to the bottom of the totem pole.

PLAY BALL

Tops of plastic bleach containers are used for this interesting and imaginative game. Each youngster is equipped with at least one container for catching and throwing purposes. A table tennis ball is effectively used for indoor play. As a youngster's skill increases, the size of the container may be cut down to increase the challenge.

MAKE IT WITH FELT

It is desirable to cut your patterns from wrapping paper prior to cutting out the felt. These paper patterns should be placed on the felt material to be cut and held in place with several straight pins. Cut with scissors. The decorative pillows are stitched with a running stitch along the edges with a large darning needle and a decorative thread.

When the two sections are almost completely together, the units are stuffed with shredded foam rubber or any other appropriate materials. The tote bag is a single layer of material with the bottom stitched on. Add handles and side pockets as desired.

SPATTER PAINTING

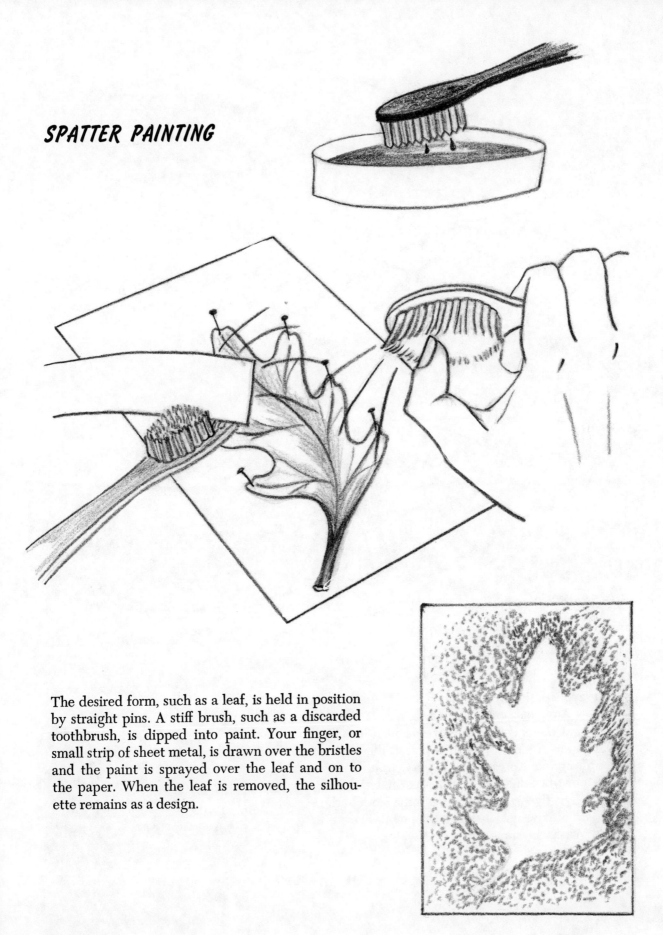

The desired form, such as a leaf, is held in position by straight pins. A stiff brush, such as a discarded toothbrush, is dipped into paint. Your finger, or small strip of sheet metal, is drawn over the bristles and the paint is sprayed over the leaf and on to the paper. When the leaf is removed, the silhouette remains as a design.

WAX BATIK

A crayon design is developed on white drawing paper. Any color crayon can be used. It is important that the crayon coating be applied heavily to the paper. A piece of cloth is placed directly over the design and pressed with a hot iron. The wax will penetrate into the cloth. The material is dip dyed. The dye will permeate into the cloth in those areas that have not absorbed the crayon. Permit to dry. Wash out crayon with hot water.

TIE DYEING

Small sections of a white cloth are gathered into lumps and tied tightly with string. The entire tied cloth is then dipped into a cold water dye. Remove and permit to dry. Remove string. The dye will penetrate only those areas which have been exposed. The areas which have been tightly tied will retain the original color of the cloth, thereby creating an overall design. If unused cloth is employed, it should be washed to remove any sizing it may contain as this would prevent effective color penetration.

ENCAUSTIC PAINTING

Small pieces of crayon of various colors are individually melted. Use a pencil with the eraser end covered with a cloth that is held together with a rubber band. Dip the covered end into the hot wax and transfer to a sheet of heavy drawing paper. This exciting method of painting produces varied and interesting effects. This craft also provides utilization of materials which might normally be discarded.

Holiday Craft Activities

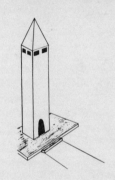

LINCOLN'S BIRTHDAY
February 12

Abraham Lincoln was born in a log cabin in Hardin County, Kentucky. His father, who had lived in several places in Kentucky, moved to Spencer County, Indiana in 1816. They continued to live there until Abraham was twenty-one. The next move was to Illinois where he worked as a farm laborer for a period of time. One of his first opportunities to show his leadership occurred in 1832 when he was chosen Captain of a company of volunteers who fought in the Black Hawk Indian war. After this war he settled in New Salem where he became a partner in a general store. His outside activities included positions as the local postmaster and deputy surveyor. His first political position was as a State Legislator at the age of twenty-five. The capital was moved to Springfield in 1839. Lincoln had been licensed to practice law and decided to set up a practice in the Capital.

By 1846 he had been elected a Representative to Congress. Young Lincoln was opposed to the extension of slavery into free territory. The Republican party was formed in Illinois in 1856. At this convention he made a very strong speech against slavery.

In 1858 the Republican party selected Abraham Lincoln as its candidate for the United States Senate. His Democratic opponent was Stephen A. Douglas. These two men debated the issues with each other on several occasions. These debates helped to make Lincoln a national figure of prominence.

In 1860, at the Chicago Convention, he was nominated for the Presidency of the United States. He was elected in 1861. The Civil War began about a month after he became president. He was reelected President in 1864 and met his tragic death on April 14, 1865. John Wilkes Booth, an actor, shot Lincoln while he was attending Ford's Theater in Washington. The next morning, Lincoln died.

Most of the States observe the anniversay of his birth as a legal holiday. Today Lincoln is considered as one of the great presidents. School children celebrate the occasion through programs and activities of many types.

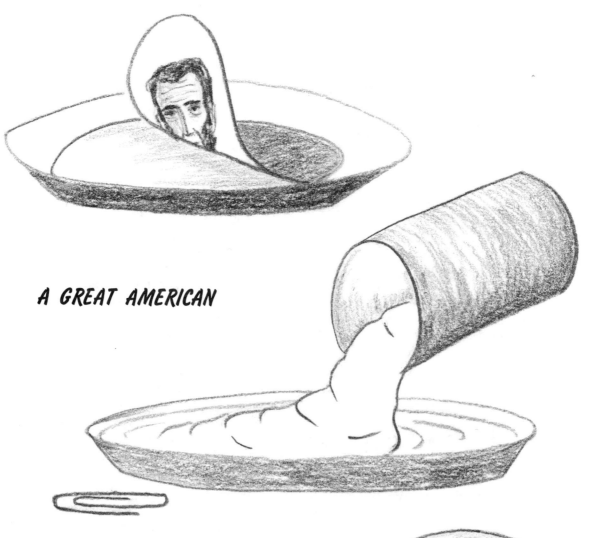

A GREAT AMERICAN

A picture of Abraham Lincoln is cut from a magazine and placed *face down* in the center of a paper plate. Plaster of Paris is mixed with water to the consistency of heavy cream. Fill paper plate with plaster of Paris. Place a paper clip half way into the plaster and towards the top of the picture. Permit to dry. Remove the paper plate from the plaster (the picture will stick to the plaster of Paris). Carefully smooth edges of plaster and spray with clear lacquer.

118

SILHOUETTE PICTURES

Cut out silhouette of Lincoln from construction paper. Place on glass that you have removed from picture frame. Tape cut out silhouette on glass. Using black oil paint and pen outline silhouette on the glass. Remove original picture and with brush and black paint, fill in the outline. Remount glass in picture frame with painted side in. Cut sheet of aluminum foil and mount behind the glass. Replace the backing of the picture.

119

Students may be encouraged to print the Gettysburg Address on the regular classroom blackboard. This will serve as the guideline for the student's individual work. Alphabet macaroni are glued to pieces of stiff black cardboard. Letter and word recognition can be enhanced with this technique. Teachers are encouraged to expand this method by individualizing students' work.

ST. VALENTINE'S DAY
February 14

There are three St. Valentines associated with February 14. One is described as a priest of Rome, the second as Bishop of Interamna, and very little is known of the third man who suffered martyrdom. All these men were buried in the Flaminian Way in the second half of the third century.

There are many versions as to how St. Valentine's Day originated. One group believes that it originated from the belief that birds mate on February 14. Another group believes that it had its beginning based on this day as being sacred to lovers.

Another theory is that it had its origin in the Roman feast of the Lupercalia. The names of young women and men were deposited in a box and then were drawn by chance. The men and women paired by this method were expected to sort of look after one another for a year. The clergy did not like this method so they substituted the names of Saints for the names of the young people. The young people drawing the names of the Saints were expected to emulate them for a period of a year.

Out of this lottery drawing developed the custom of the boy and girl exchanging presents. This practice in time changed to the form of Valentine cards. Valentine cards are made by children in school and the messages recorded on the cards are also done by them. Cards may also be purchased in many different forms and varieties.

MY VALENTINE

Make them big, make them small as you wish for your valentine. Use construction paper, card paper and buttons and beads for eyes and pipe cleaners for whiskers. Paint features with tempera paints and serve them up as My Valentine.

WOVEN VALENTINES

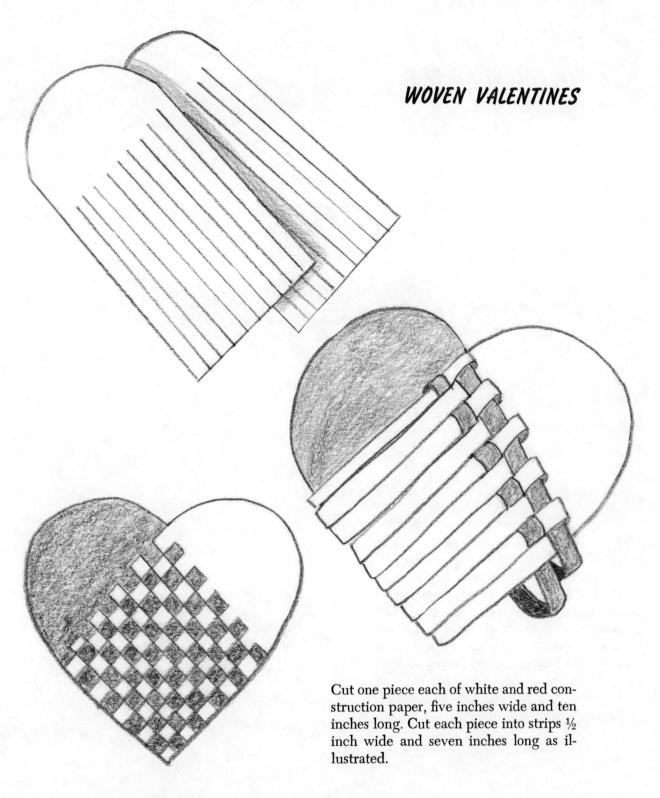

Cut one piece each of white and red construction paper, five inches wide and ten inches long. Cut each piece into strips ½ inch wide and seven inches long as illustrated.

Weave at right angles to one another, pasting each end securely. Trim unwoven sections into heart shapes. Add message with marking pen, if desired.

MY VALENTINE TRAY

An effective serving tray can be made from ¼ inch plywood or tempered masonite. Make the tray according to your desired dimensions. Two ¼ inch dowels are glued lengthwise to the base. The handles can be from twisted wire or heavy rope. Glue in place. Four wooden beads are fastened to the bottom as legs. A large heart cut from construction paper is glued in the center of the tray. Shellac is used for the finish.

VALENTINE DECORATION

A large grapefruit supported by a twenty penny common spike with the head embedded in a glob of plaster of Paris, provides the base for this interesting centerpiece. Heart-shaped features are cut from construction paper and glued into place. Toothpicks topped by colorful gum drops are embedded into the grapefruit.

BE MY VALENTINE

A four inch styrofoam ball with features cut from construction paper and pasted on, forms the head of this valentine mobile. Antennae are from pipe cleaners with gum drops fastened to the ends. Hearts are cut from construction paper with slits running half way down the middle so that they are crosslapped, therefore forming the body. A thin string is threaded through the styrofoam ball by first creating a hole with a coat hanger. A knot is added to prevent slippage. The bottom end of the string is glued to the intersection of the cross-lapped hearts. Suitable expressions can be written on the surfaces of the hearts with marking pens.

126

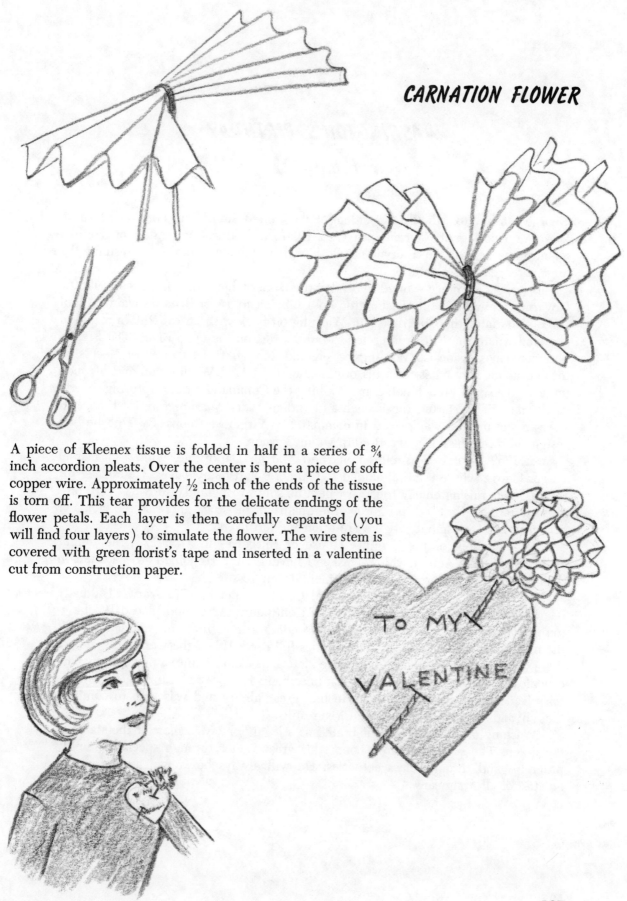

CARNATION FLOWER

A piece of Kleenex tissue is folded in half in a series of ¾ inch accordion pleats. Over the center is bent a piece of soft copper wire. Approximately ½ inch of the ends of the tissue is torn off. This tear provides for the delicate endings of the flower petals. Each layer is then carefully separated (you will find four layers) to simulate the flower. The wire stem is covered with green florist's tape and inserted in a valentine cut from construction paper.

TO MY
VALENTINE

WASHINGTON'S BIRTHDAY
February 22

George Washington, the first president of the United States, was born on a farm in Westmoreland County, Virginia, in 1732. His formal education was slight. He had talent in mathematics and surveying. Both of these talents were used in farming the huge acreage of his plantations.

Britain and France wanted to occupy the Upper Ohio Valley in the early 1750's. Governor Dinwidde sent Washington on a mission to assert Britain's claim. About three years later the Governor sent Washington back with an expedition to guard the land where the British intended to build a fort on the Ohio River. The French had taken possession, so Washington erected another fort called Fort Necessity, located about fifty miles from his original sight. In 1754 Washington and his men ambushed a small French detachment killing the Commander and capturing several of the men. This started the French and Indian Wars. Washington, by 1755, had risen in stature and was placed in command of Virginia's troops. By 1758 he had resigned his commission and retired to Mount Vernon.

In 1759 George Washington married Martha Dandridge, widow of Daniel Parker Curtis, whose estate included 15,000 acres and many slaves. He farmed for several years raising chiefly tobacco which he sold to England. He was a very progressive farmer. He tried to improve the quality of his stock, increase the yields of his fields, and experiment with crop rotation and fertilizers.

As a member of the Virginia House of Burgesses in 1759–1774, he fought against the Stamp Act and the Townshend Revenue Act. He joined other leaders in their cry for the development of a Continental Congress.

By the time the second Continental Congress met in 1775 war had already begun near Boston. Congress created the Continental Army and placed Washington in command. England responded by sending a huge force to America to fight the newly formed army. Many hard battles followed. When the war finally ended, there was agitation for consolidating the victorious Colonies into a new nation. The Colonies acted and George Washington became its first president in 1789. Washington's leadership was outstanding. He had great ability and was able to combine thought and action into attaining desired results.

Washington's birthday is celebrated as a legal holiday in most of the states of the union. The school children honor this great leader through special assembly programs and through class activities. He will always be known as one of the greatest of all Americans.

MILITARY HATS

A plastic jug is cut approximately five and a half inches from the bottom, using the top position as the crown of the hat. Fasten a piece of stiff cardboard that has been cut into the shape of a visor. This visor can be fastened with tabs and stapled to the inside of the crown. The plume is made from strips of construction paper and is glued and inserted into the pour spout of the jug. A band of construction paper is stapled around the hairline of the hat. An elastic band is cut and each end stapled to the inside of the hat. Additional ornamentations may be added as desired.

Heavy cardboard, or masonite that has been painted black, is used as the backing for this patriotic message. Alphabet letters that have been laid out on an identical sized paper to insure proper spacing and centering, are transferred and glued to the painted backing. A string is attached for hanging.

Cut out the silhouette of a tree from black construction paper, including trunk and branches. Paste the cut out tree on white construction paper. Crumple small pieces of colored tissue paper and paste on branches for foliage.

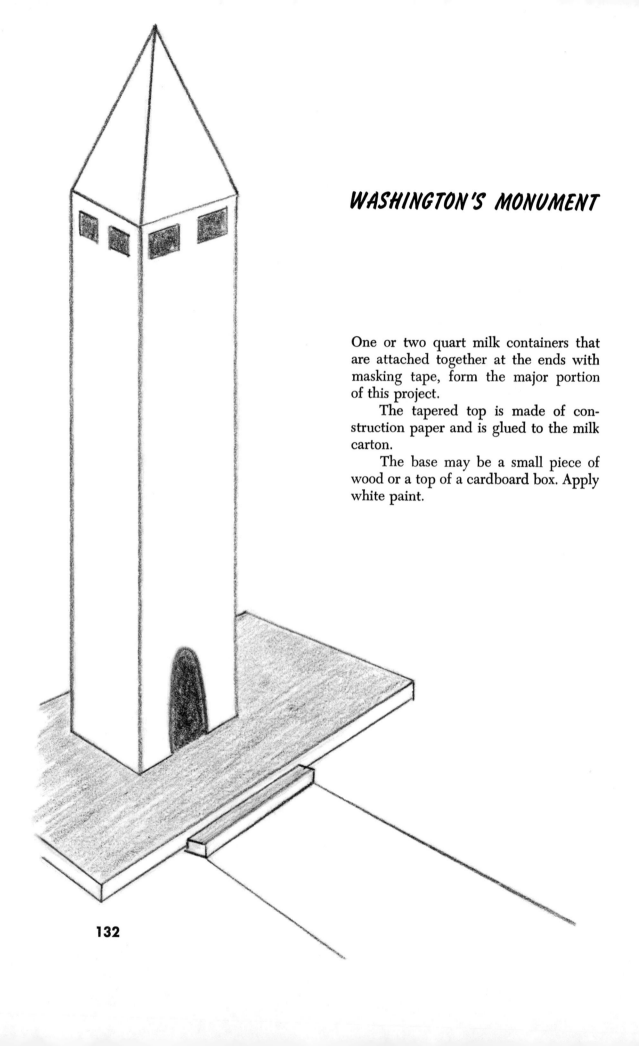

WASHINGTON'S MONUMENT

One or two quart milk containers that are attached together at the ends with masking tape, form the major portion of this project.

The tapered top is made of construction paper and is glued to the milk carton.

The base may be a small piece of wood or a top of a cardboard box. Apply white paint.

132

EASTER
March or April

Easter is now celebrated on the Sunday after the first full moon following the equinox. During the early years of the Christian church, there was no general agreement as to a specific date for celebration. The resurrection took place during the Jewish Passover Celebration. The Jewish Calendar which was used at the time marked the date as the fourteenth day of the month Nisan. The Calendar had peculiarities and therefore the date did not always fall on the same day of the week. Variations occurred which caused the celebration to vary as much as thirty days.

Christianity teaches that Jesus rose from the dead on the third day following crucifixion "Sunday," the first day of the week. There was disagreement between the Christians and the Jews as to whether the celebration should be on Sunday or on the day of the date of the Passover. The council of NICAEA which met in 325 decided that the church would celebrate the occasion on the same day throughout the church. They finally decided that the date should be established as the Sunday after the first full moon following the spring equinox. Easter as a result of this decision now falls between March 22 and April 25.

The Roman and Greek Churches developed elaborate rituals for the celebration of Easter. The Protestants, however, abhorred religious ceremonials and, therefore, did not celebrate the occasion. The custom in the Protestant churches has changed in the past half century and now virtually all denominations observe Easter.

During the Civil War nonritualistic churches began to celebrate Easter. The war caused the loss of many lives and resulted in bereaved homes. The Easter season was to serve as a reminder, for those who had lost dear ones in the war, of the promise of resurrection as given in the story of Christ who had risen.

Most churches now decorate with flowers for the Easter service. The Bermuda lily which blooms in the spring is the flower most generally used. Because this flower is used so extensively at Easter, it has become known as the Easter lily.

The egg has become a symbol of the resurrection because it holds the seed of new life. People in the early church did not eat eggs during Lent. They were served on Easter Sunday. The egg as a symbol of new life as well as the coloring of eggs is of very old origin.

ALL FOR EGGS

Give hard boiled eggs a wash coat of water color. Cut strips of colored paper from construction paper or cut odd shaped pieces and glue on eggs. Braid, colored string, or other materials may also be used to add decorative effects.

FUNNY BUNNY

Paint the salt or oatmeal box with a wash coat of water color. Ears of construction paper may be enhanced by using colored crayon or water colors. Features may be painted on or pieces of felt, colored paper, yarn or string may be glued to the box. Feathers or colored paper are glued around the bottom of the box for added effect.

135

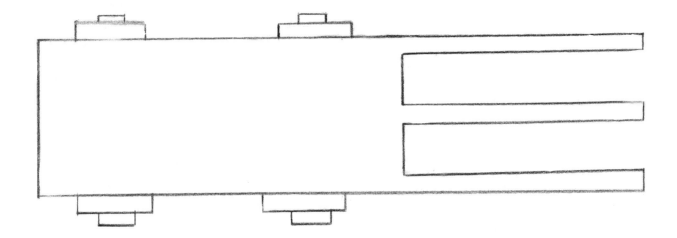

A piece of ¼ inch plywood forms the bed of this bunny wagon with two sections cut out as illustrated to receive two rabbits that have been cut from heavy cardboard. An egg container is placed on the bed portion of this wagon. The yokes are attached to the two rabbits by strips of construction paper. Buttons or circular dishes are glued to the edges of the wagon bed. Decorate as desired.

BUNNY WAGONS

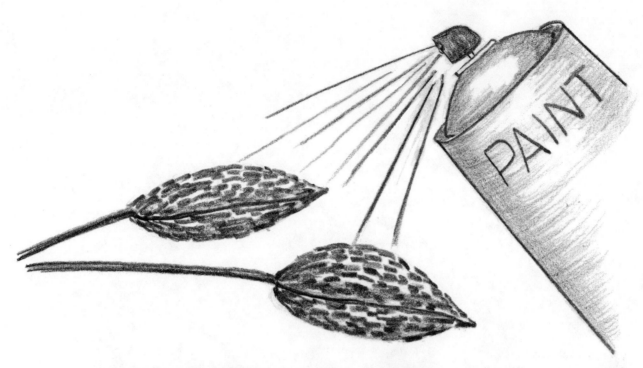

EASTER DECORATION FROM NATURE

Collect dried leaves, seed pods, twigs, branches, pine cones, and the like. Spray with various colored spray paints and assemble to form a decorative centerpiece for your table.

137

BIRDS IN THE CAGE

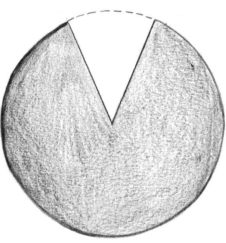

Cut two six inch circles from heavy cardboard and punch holes of the same diameter as straws around the edges of each circle. Space holes ¾ of an inch apart on center. Attach soda straws with glue as illustrated. Cut an eight inch diameter circle from construction paper and remove pie shape segment as illustrated. Glue edges of remaining segment together to form cone. Attach cone to top with glue. Cut out silhouettes of birds from construction paper. Decorate with paint, attach thread and hang from top of cage. Add beads, and the like to cage for decoration.

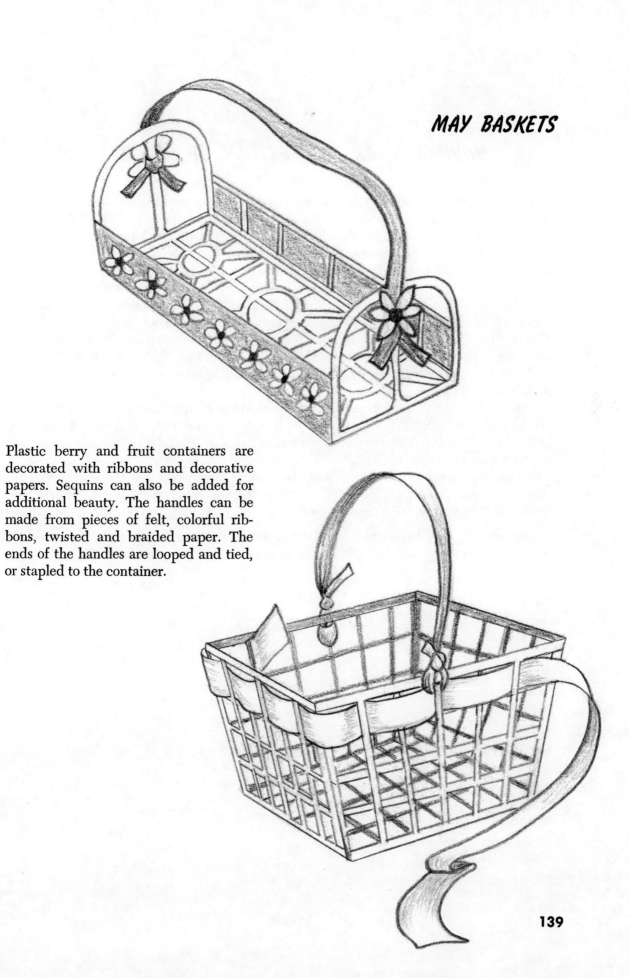

Plastic berry and fruit containers are decorated with ribbons and decorative papers. Sequins can also be added for additional beauty. The handles can be made from pieces of felt, colorful ribbons, twisted and braided paper. The ends of the handles are looped and tied, or stapled to the container.

HANUKKAH, OR THE FESTIVAL OF LIGHTS

The Jewish festival known as Hanukkah may be known by several other names such as Channukah, Feast of Dedication, the Feast of the Maccabees, and the Festival of Lights. It was instituted by the elders of the congregation of Israel in the year 165 B.C. Antiochus Epiphanes, three years earlier, had desecrated the temple and set up a pagan altar in the temple and offered sacrifices to Zeus Olympius. The Jews recaptured the temple and built new fires at the altar. They also lit the candles and the lamps. The Jews celebrated by sacrifices and sang songs similar to those on the Feast of the Tabernacles. The Talmud describes the occasion as the Feast of Illumination. Perhaps the name is derived from the illumination produced by lighting eight lamps on the first night and the elimination of one light each succeeding night, or beginning with one light the first night and lighting an additional light a night until eight lights are lit.

A small bottle of consecrated oil was found in the temple after its desecration. It had not been polluted by the pagans. It was used in the recaptured temple and lasted for eight days. The Jews used elaborate lamps and candlesticks made from silver, bronze and copper.

The lamps used in the homes were placed near the door so that they could be seen by persons passing by. Each light represented a member of the family. When the lamps were lighted all persons recited:

BLESSED BY THE LORD OUR GOD, KING OF THE UNIVERSE, WHO HAS SANCTIFIED US BY THY COMMANDMENTS AND ENJOINED US TO KINDLE THE HANUKKAH LAMP.

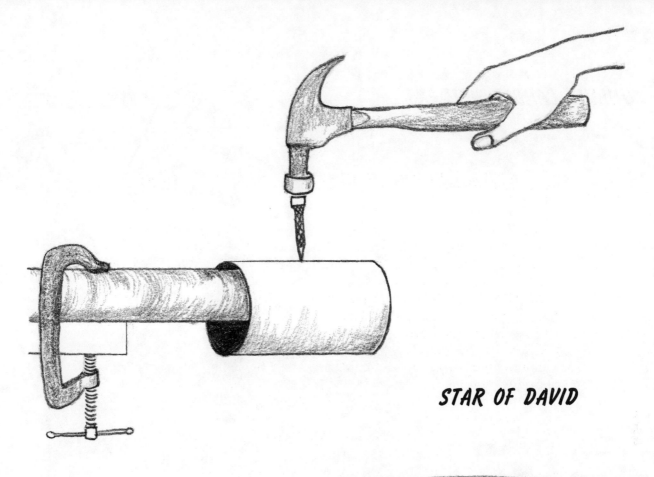

STAR OF DAVID

A large size tin can with the label and glue removed from the outside forms the basic form for the symbolic representation of the Jewish religion. The six pointed star is created by a series of small lines or center punch holes that are produced by placing the can over a large wooden object such as the end of a baseball bat. A candle is placed in the bottom to produce the necessary light to illuminate through the small holes the six pointed star.

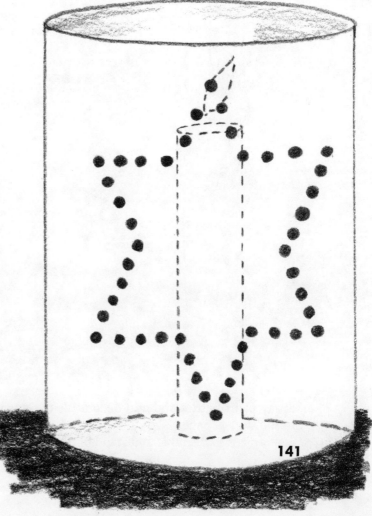

UNIQUE CANDLE HOLDERS

Spray paint bottles and add decorative designs with oil paint. To the mouth of the bottle add a paper cup as illustrated. Decorate and set in your candles. Add a centerpiece to the table and stand bottles in appropriate position.

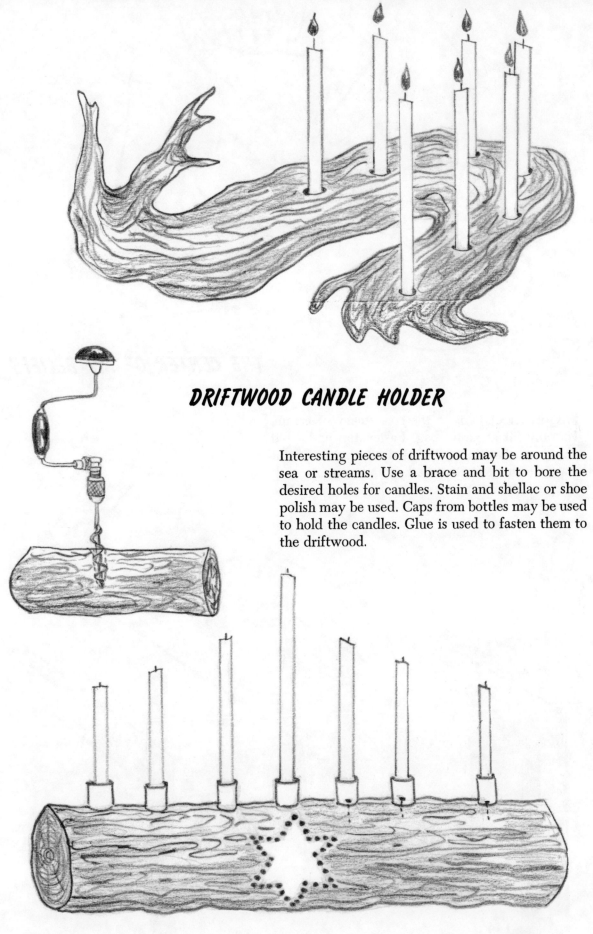

DRIFTWOOD CANDLE HOLDER

Interesting pieces of driftwood may be around the sea or streams. Use a brace and bit to bore the desired holes for candles. Stain and shellac or shoe polish may be used. Caps from bottles may be used to hold the candles. Glue is used to fasten them to the driftwood.

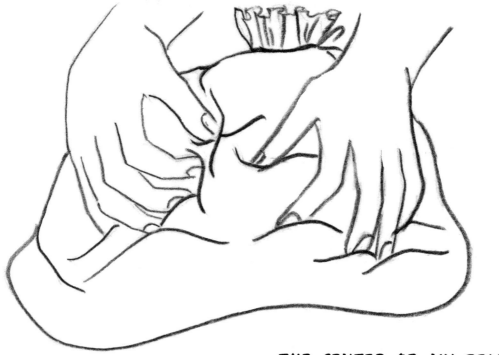

THE CENTER OF MY BELIEFS

Mix plaster of Paris to the consistency of cream. Partially fill a plastic bag. Fasten top and mold plaster of Paris into the desired shape. Permit plaster to harden. Remove bag and decorate with tempera paints. Spray with clear lacquer. Use during this festive occasion.

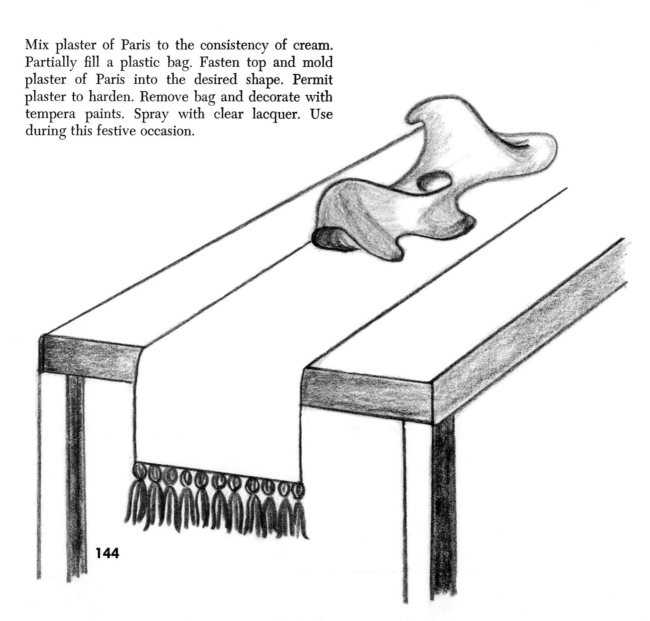

144

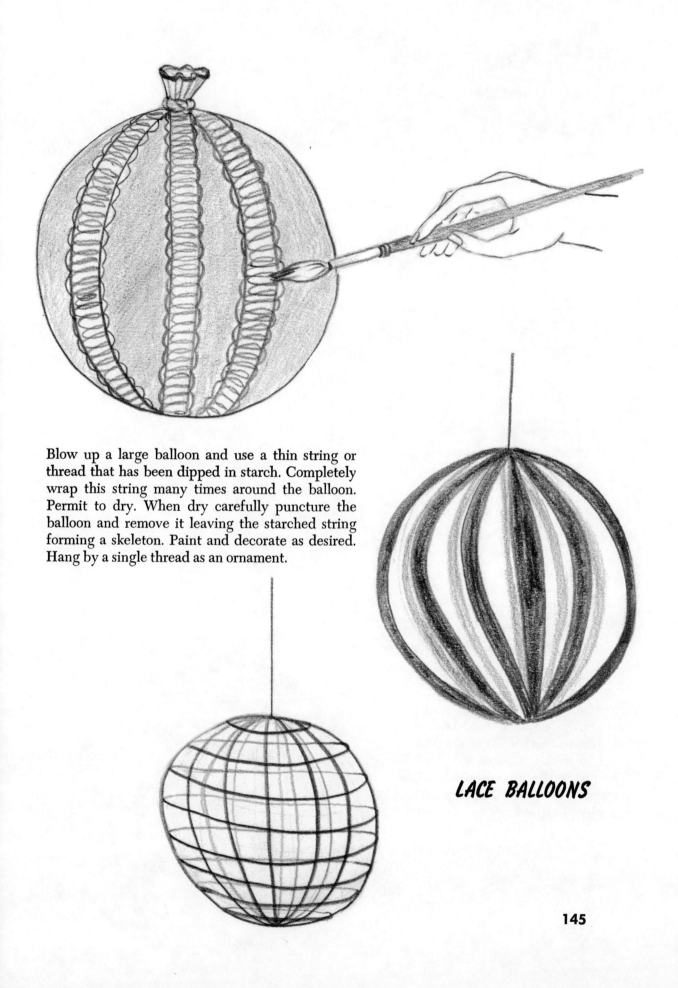

Blow up a large balloon and use a thin string or thread that has been dipped in starch. Completely wrap this string many times around the balloon. Permit to dry. When dry carefully puncture the balloon and remove it leaving the starched string forming a skeleton. Paint and decorate as desired. Hang by a single thread as an ornament.

LACE BALLOONS

145

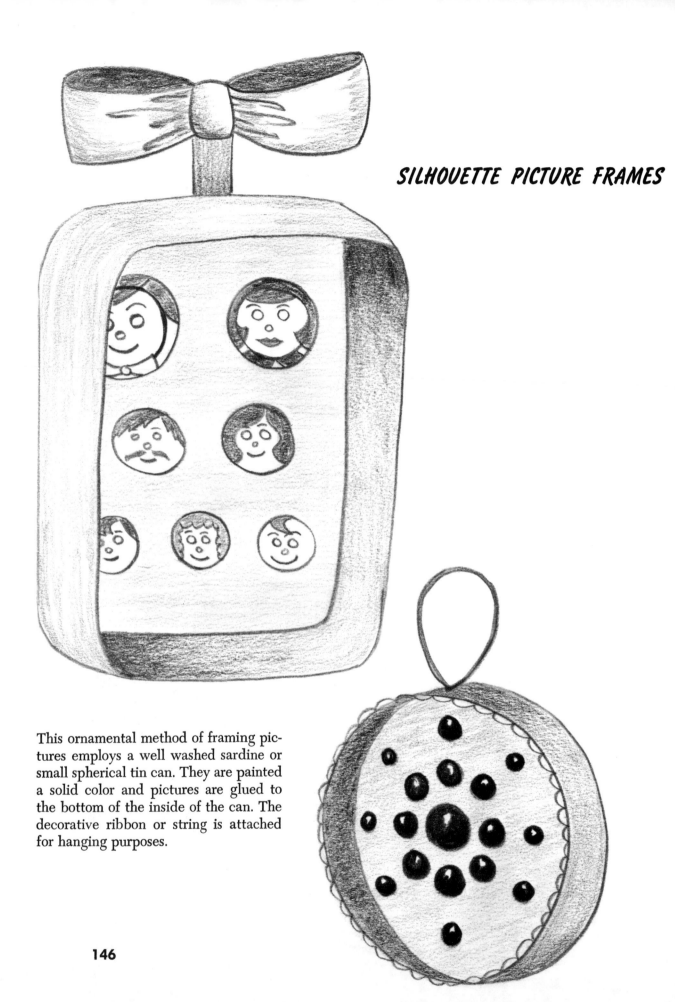

This ornamental method of framing pictures employs a well washed sardine or small spherical tin can. They are painted a solid color and pictures are glued to the bottom of the inside of the can. The decorative ribbon or string is attached for hanging purposes.

146

MOTHER'S DAY
Second Sunday in May

The custom of celebrating motherhood is very old. It began with the Greeks who worshipped Cybele, the mother of gods. The celebrations we hold today honoring mothers on the second Sunday in May, however, are entirely different and are of comparatively recent origin.

The observance of Mother's Day as we know it began in Philadelphia in May, 1907. Miss Anna M. Jarvis, who had the idea that all sons and daughters should pay tribute to their mothers at least once a year, arranged a special church service and notified those who came to honor mothers to wear white carnations. The following year other churches in the Philadelphia area adopted the idea. They later agreed to honor mothers each year on the second Sunday in May.

By 1911 the observance had spread to all of the states and had also been observed in many foreign nations.

The House of Representatives in May of 1913 passed a resolution calling for all federal officials to wear a white carnation on the second Sunday of May in observation of Mother's Day. In 1914 Congress recognized the day and asked that the President request all federal officials to display the American flag on all federal buildings. President Wilson was the first president to issue such a proclamation. He went beyond the original request of Congress by asking all people to display flags on their homes. The proclamation is now a tradition and is issued each year by the president.

Today white carnations are worn by persons whose mothers have passed away. Red carnations are worn by others. In many observances the custom of white and red carnations are now giving way to white and red flowers in general.

Sons and daughters traditionally give mother a present on Mother's Day. When the tradition began, it was usually in the form of a card, the most popular being a reproduction of Whistler's portrait of his mother. The United States government in 1934 issued a three cent stamp bearing the reproduction of the Whistler painting.

PENDANTS

Use a one and one-half inch styrofoam ball, beauty pins, seed beads and sequins. The entire surface of the styrofoam ball is completely covered and each beauty pin is threaded to two seed beads and one sequin as illustrated, in patterns that are pleasing to you. The two ends of a colored string are forced into the styrofoam ball and glued into place. The string should be approximately twenty-four inches long and will substitute for a necklace.

LOVE BEADS

Cut a large triangle shaped strip of paper. Roll from the large end to the small end around a toothpick. Add glue or paste as you roll. When each bead is completely rolled up, remove toothpick. Thread these beads on a string, adding other types of beads between each handmade bead. Fasten ends together to form necklace.

149

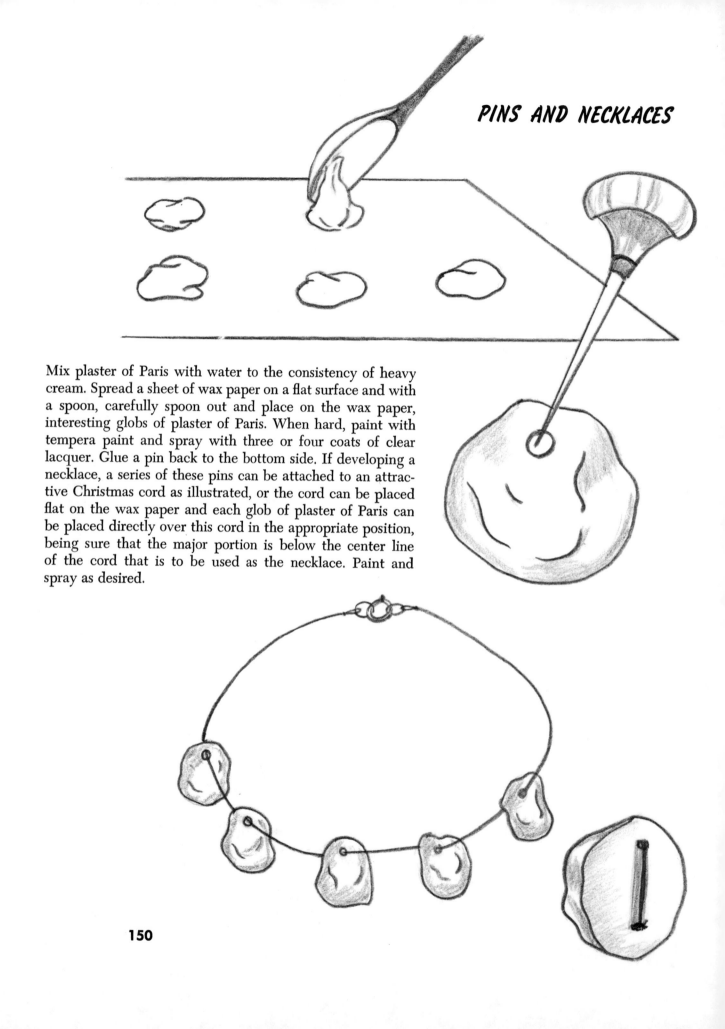

Mix plaster of Paris with water to the consistency of heavy cream. Spread a sheet of wax paper on a flat surface and with a spoon, carefully spoon out and place on the wax paper, interesting globs of plaster of Paris. When hard, paint with tempera paint and spray with three or four coats of clear lacquer. Glue a pin back to the bottom side. If developing a necklace, a series of these pins can be attached to an attractive Christmas cord as illustrated, or the cord can be placed flat on the wax paper and each glob of plaster of Paris can be placed directly over this cord in the appropriate position, being sure that the major portion is below the center line of the cord that is to be used as the necklace. Paint and spray as desired.

150

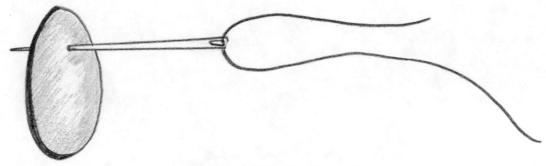

SEED NECKLACE

Cantaloupe and pumpkin seeds that have been previously tinted with vegetable dyes form the basic units. While still moist after tinting, string with nylon thread and attach brass ring and clasp. To add luster spray after threading with plastic spray.

151

KITTY KATS

Mother cat is made from an inch and a half thick soft pine board that has been cut to the desired dimensions and shape. A coping saw is best used for the curved sections. All surfaces are sanded smooth. The head is a carefully selected stone that is glued to the top portion of the wooden body. Features are painted on using enamel paints. A felt pen can be used for fine details. Tail and ears are made from leather, or stiff paper, and glued into place. Whiskers are obtained from an old corn broom and glued to the stone. Other details are added as desired. The kittens are self-explanatory.

TOTE BOX

Virtually any size cardboard box can be made into an attractive tote box for various uses. The outside of the box is gaily decorated with paints, wallpaper, Christmas wrappings and/or other imaginative means. Holes are punched as illustrated along the sides. These holes should be slightly larger than the rope that is going to be used for handles. The ends are brought together at the top and held in position with masking tape. Colorful cord wrapping is placed over the tape to form the handle. Shellac or lacquer may be used as a final finish.

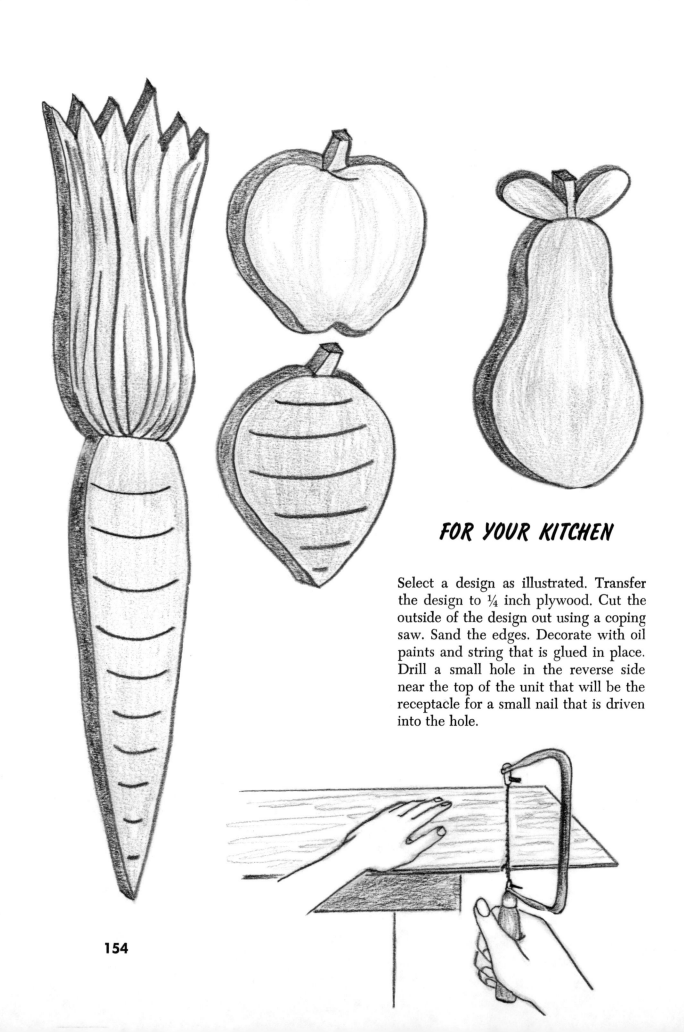

FOR YOUR KITCHEN

Select a design as illustrated. Transfer the design to ¼ inch plywood. Cut the outside of the design out using a coping saw. Sand the edges. Decorate with oil paints and string that is glued in place. Drill a small hole in the reverse side near the top of the unit that will be the receptacle for a small nail that is driven into the hole.

HOT POT PAD

Masonite or wood may be used as a base. Use coping saw to cut bamboo pole into ½ inch lengths. Glue the lengths vertically to the base.

½"

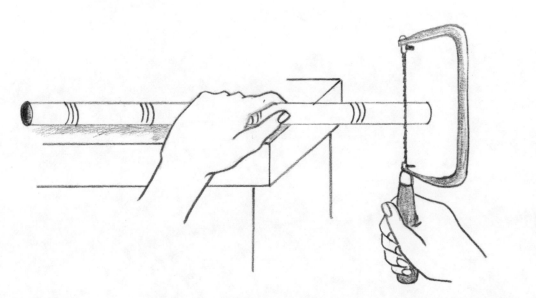

155

FATHER'S DAY
Third Sunday in June

There is some doubt as to how or where the idea of Father's Day was born. Some give Mrs. John Bruce Dodd of Spokane, Washington the honor. In 1909 Mrs. Dodd conceived the idea that there should be a day set aside for honoring fathers. The idea probably was the result of Mrs. Dodd's desire to pay tribute to her own father who had reared the family after her mother had died.

Mrs. Dodd contacted the Reverend Conrad Bluhm, President of the Spokane Ministerial Association, and asked that his association give consideration to recognizing the third Sunday in June as Father's Day. The Association acted favorably on Mrs. Dodd's proposal and celebrated the day in Spokane in June 1910. The sons and daughters were requested to wear red roses if their fathers were living. They were requested to wear white roses if their fathers had passed away.

The idea of Father's Day in Spokane received very little, if any, out of state publicity. A group in Chicago in 1911 and a group in Vancouver, Washington, in 1913, celebrated what they referred to as Father's Day. Both of these groups laid claim to having originated the idea.

The recognition of Father's Day was very slow and even the groups that did recognize the day, celebrated it on different days and months of the year. Several early attempts were made in Congress to establish a definite date for Father's Day. These early attempts ended in failure.

Merchants are always aware of the business possibilities involved in designated holidays. When Mother's Day was formed, the confectioners responded by offering candy specially wrapped for the occasion. They were also ready when Father's Day was recognized. Presents to father today vary greatly but in many cases the gifts consist of ties and shirts and other personalized gifts.

PASTE ONS

Design with a flair, paint macaroni with tempera paint and using white glue, fasten to tin cans that have been painted with oil paint. Also try your imagination on flat sheets of heavy paper, frame and hang as pictures.

157

WEIGHTY FRIENDS

Interesting shaped stones and/or buttons make delightful paper weights. Cut feet for bottom that permits legs and appendages to show. Glue to stone or button and add features with paint.

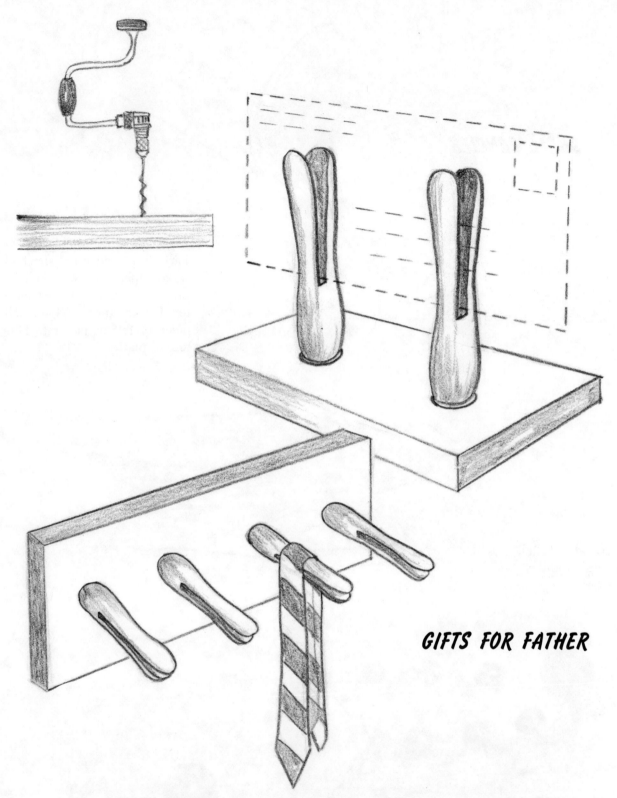

GIFTS FOR FATHER

Use a ¾ inch wood block as a base. A small saw, or coping saw, is used to cut off the heads of these ordinary clothes pins. Drill holes in base, insert and glue. Smaller children may glue the pins directly to the base. Paint or decorate to suit your fancy.

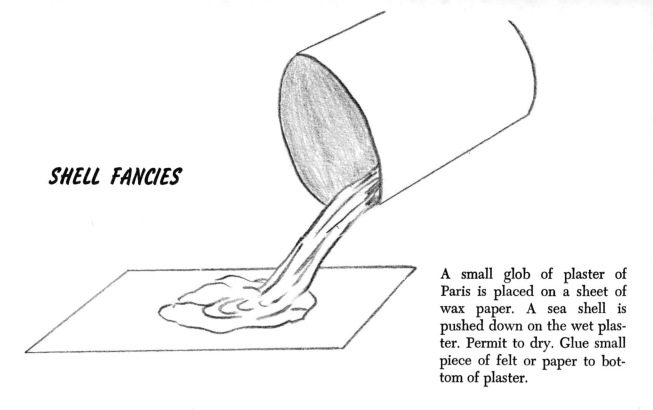

SHELL FANCIES

A small glob of plaster of Paris is placed on a sheet of wax paper. A sea shell is pushed down on the wet plaster. Permit to dry. Glue small piece of felt or paper to bottom of plaster.

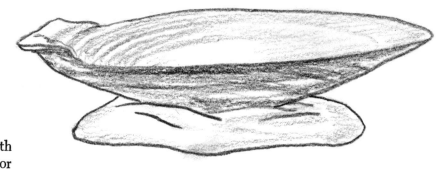

Decorate shell with beads, sequins and/or glitter.

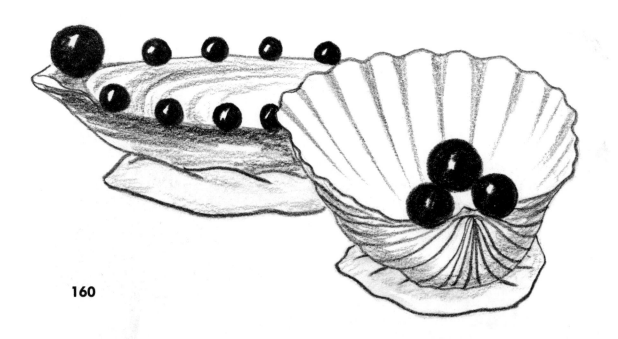

QUACK-QUACKS

The duck is constructed by cutting a circle as illustrated from a piece of ½ inch soft pine that is cut off to accept the spring clothespin which is glued to form the body. The head is likewise a partial circle that is also glued to the upper portion of the spring clothespin. The feet are formed by cutting a small Vee groove at the base. Wings are formed by using a piece of construction paper and glued to the side of the body. The same procedure is used for the penguin with necessary body contour changes. The penguin hat is developed from construction paper and glued to the head.

161

FOR THE DECORATIVE FLARE

Use a strip of burlap approximately twelve inches by eighteen inches that has been wrapped and sewn at each end around a ¼ inch dowel as illustrated. Glue the burlap on a firm backing such as heavy cardboard. Pieces of twigs, cane and strips of balsa wood are glued to the burlap to form the basic design as desired. Sections of this design can be painted with oil paint to enhance the motif.

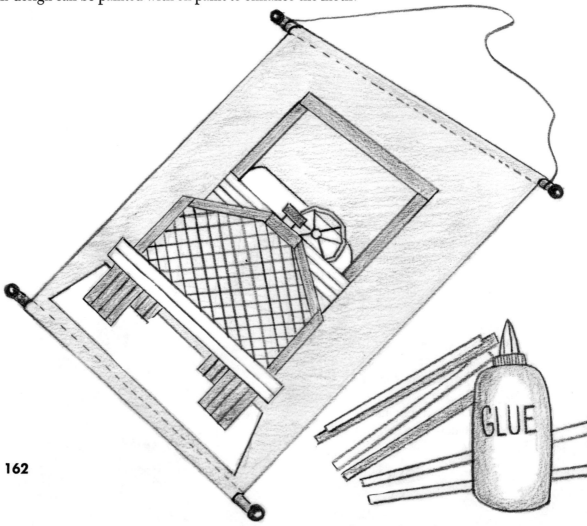

SHELLY WEIGHT

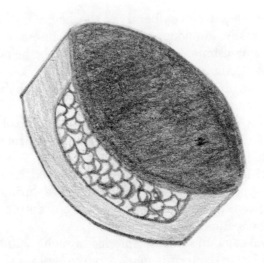

Fill a small round-shaped dish with tiny shells of all types or other suitable material. Cut cardboard and felt to fit. Glue on bottom. Let dry—invert and enjoy.

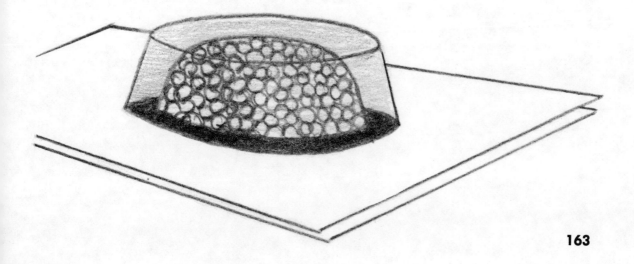

163

HALLOWEEN
October 31

Halloween today is celebrated on October 31. Its origin, however, began with the Druids centuries before the dawn of the Christian Era. Many of the ancient rites were brought to this country from Europe. They no longer have mystic significance. Today the festivities are on the fun side and are celebrated mostly by the young people.

The Druids considered November 1 as the beginning of the year and celebrated by holding a festival in honor of the sun god. Fires were lit in his honor. The Druids believed that punishment of the wicked could be helped by giving gifts and offering prayers to the god.

The story of the origin of the jack-o'-lanterns probably began in Ireland. According to the story a very stingy man named Jack could not get into heaven because of his stinginess and could not get into hell because of the practical jokes he played on the devil. He, therefore, was condemned to roam the earth with his lantern until the final judgment day.

In the early history of the world it was believed that witches and ghosts existed. They were supposed to have been most active during Halloween. Persecutions for witchcraft were quite common in the seventeenth century in the colonies of Massachusetts, Connecticut and Virginia.

The families who came to settle in America brought with them their Halloween customs. Today the jack-o'-lantern is made from pumpkins instead of large turnips as used in Scotland.

Halloween today is regarded as a time for fun rather than a time for serious consultation with the magic oracles as in the past. Children wear masks and fancy costumes today when they roam the neighborhoods asking for candy, apples, fruit or other delicacies. This is a real fun day in the lives of the very young.

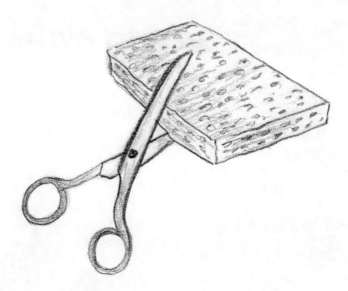

Rubber sponges of various colors are cut into interesting patterns and designs and glued with rubber cement to form your own rubber mask. Rubber cement should be applied to both surfaces which are to be glued. Permit both surfaces to dry before pressing together. This contact method of gluing eliminates the necessity of holding the pieces together until dry.

HALLOWEEN HATS

Deep aluminum cake pans decorated with paint, sequins, construction paper, paper cups and odds and ends add much to the occasion. A length of elastic string can be used to help hold on the hat. Add your own ideas for individuality.

WITCHES AND GOBLINS

Paper plates decorated with paints and felt marking pens, construction paper, yarn and pipe cleaners form the basic materials required for these Halloween faces. Create your own monsters by providing opportunity for individual expression on the part of each youngster. Let's see who can make the scariest one.

Cut the brim from the crown of an old hat. Decorate the crown using buttons, sequins and glitter. Add a decorative branch or twig to the center. Colored string may be used as a binding around the raw edge. Add your own originality to this hat for all occasions.

168

HALLOWEEN CUTOUTS

Individually designed to represent the symbols of Hallow-een, these units are constructed from black and orange construction paper.

Scissors, paste, and marking pens are employed in the making. The child's contribution is then taped to a classroom window or other appropriate place.

169

MARBLEIZED PAPER

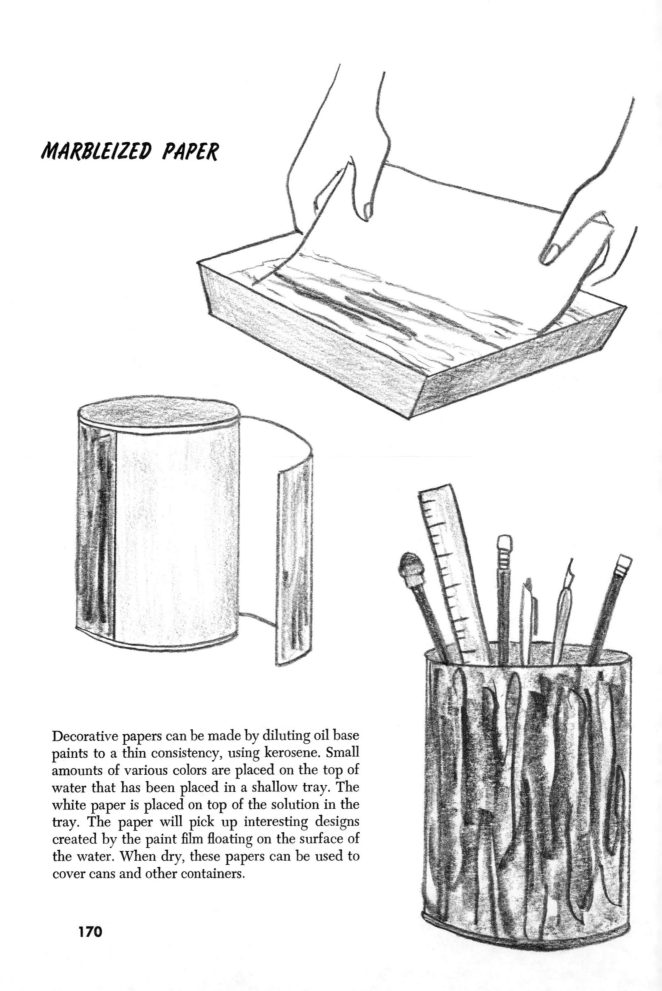

Decorative papers can be made by diluting oil base paints to a thin consistency, using kerosene. Small amounts of various colors are placed on the top of water that has been placed in a shallow tray. The white paper is placed on top of the solution in the tray. The paper will pick up interesting designs created by the paint film floating on the surface of the water. When dry, these papers can be used to cover cans and other containers.

THANKSGIVING
Fourth Thursday in November

Mrs. Sarah J. Hale, editor of the Ladies Magazine in 1827, is credited with bringing about the idea of Thanksgiving. She advocated that a special day be designated for the expression of thanks for the blessings of the year. She wrote letters to all the governors, and to the President requesting them to designate the fourth Thursday in November as a day of Thanksgiving.

The Ladies Magazine was consolidated with Godey's Lady's Book. The combined circulation was approximately 150,000. As editor of this combined publication, she wrote many editorials extolling the virtues of her proposed day of thanksgiving. Her writings bore fruit as evidenced by a proclamation issued by President Lincoln in 1863. The day designated was the fourth Thursday in November. Churches responded to the proclamation by holding services and sermons were preached relevant to the occasion.

In the early ceremonies, the families attended church and then returned home to feast on a meal featuring roast turkey and pumpkin pie. The family reunion and sumptuous dinners on Thanksgiving Day appear to have become a tradition.

In many locations the churches are decorated with products of the farm in an effort to remind people of our bountiful products so that they may appreciate their blessings.

Wild turkeys in New England were plentiful in the early days of the settlers. This is perhaps the reason that turkey became the principal part of the meal.

The first official proclamation was issued by President Washington in 1789. It was really a day of thanksgiving for the adoption of the Constitution.

Today Thanksgiving Day is celebrated throughout the entire United States. Many homes are decorated by shocks of corn, sheaves of wheat, and centerpieces of fruits and vegetables. It is truly a day for feasting and celebrating.

Make this decorative centerpiece from heavy Christmas wrapping paper or metalized foil. Fold as illustrated. Staple or glue the two ends. Sequins, glitter, stars or other suitable materials may be used to further decorate the piece.

The bibs are made from colored construction paper and the names are written on them, using either crayons or water colors. The straps for the bibs are paper on cloth and are stapled or glued to the bib.

PARTY FUN

172

GOBBLERS

Design them small, design them large, design them for your every need. A large paper bag is carefully stuffed with folded newspaper. To the bottom of the bag are glued large pieces of construction paper which have been cut as feathers. A long, narrow bag is likewise stuffed with wadded paper and is attached as illustrated to the partially open end of the first bag. The head is formed by using a smaller bag, with a hole in the side which receives the partially open end of the long thin bag which has formed the long thin neck. The head bag is tied and decorated with tempera paints. Wire coat hangers are used for large gobblers while pipe cleaners can be used for this purpose on the smaller units.

173

TOMMY TURKEY

An attractively decorated cereal box provides the center section of Tommy Turkey. The head and neck are made from heavy construction paper and inserted and glued into a slit that has been cut lengthwise through the cereal box.

Features and other decorative touches are added as desired. The tail is also made from construction paper that has been slit to simulate feathers. It is inserted in the same manner as the head and neck.

THE GOBBLER

A large orange or styrofoam ball forms the body of our Thanksgiving friend. A cork held in place by a toothpick forms the head. A piece of construction paper cut to the design of a beak has been inserted in a slit in the cork. Sequins pinned to the cork simulate the eyes. Wings are from construction paper and are glued to the sides. Toothpicks form the holders for the colorful gumdrops. The base is an inverted pie pan that is embellished with natural or artificial leaves.

PIRATE CUPS

These decorative creatures are constructed from a paper cone shaped cup that has been painted with tempera paints and sprayed with clear lacquer. Addendums are added as desired.

176

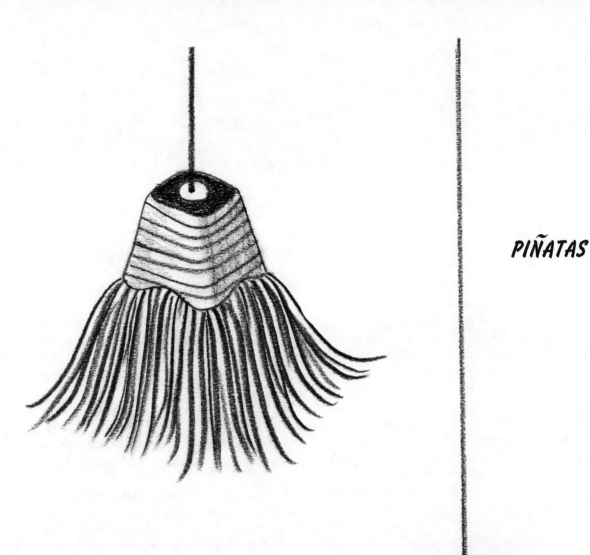

This is constructed from preformed egg cartons that have been carefully cut out. Colored string or yarn is glued on to the inside of the cup after the cup has been painted with tempera paints. Glitter can be added for an additional decorative effect. A single string is attached to the center of the Piñata for hanging purposes.

177

CHRISTMAS
December 25

Christmas is the most important day on the Christian calendar. On this day we celebrate the birth of Jesus. The exact date of the birth, however, is not known. The early Christians did not celebrate birthdays because they considered them to be heathen in origin.

The Christmas tree, as we know it, had its origin in Germany. The date is given as 1605. Martin Luther, however, is said to have taken an evergreen tree to his home many years before the 1605 date and decorated it for his children. The use of candles to decorate trees perhaps was derived from legendary sources which described the miraculous appearance of candles on trees during the Christmas season. It is believed that the Christmas tree custom was introduced into the United States by German immigrants.

The early Puritans of New England forbade the observance of Christmas. They also forbade the baking of plum puddings and mince pies because they believed the ideas were originated by heathens.

One of the first recorded Christmas celebrations in the United States took place in what is now called Bethlehem, Pennsylvania. Count Nicholas Ludwig von Zinsendorf, a Moravian, lighted a candle and led his group in a German hymn as they worshipped in a stable which was connected to the first house the group had built.

Santa Claus as a giver of Christmas presents has its derivation in the legend of St. Nicholas. According to the legend, St. Nicholas heard about three women who were unable to get married because the father was too poor to provide the dowry. St. Nicholas, according to the legend, filled three bags with gold and then threw them through the windows of the young ladies. They were soon happily married.

Thereafter any unexpected gifts were referred to as gifts from St. Nicholas. In time this idea was tied into the giving of presents at Christmas. Children also hoped to get presents so they placed their shoes and stockings near the fireplace. The Norsemen contributed to the myth when they suggested that Santa Claus entered the home through the chimney.

The idea of sending Christmas cards originated in England in 1846. In the 1870's the English firm of Marcus Ward and Company introduced the Christmas card in America. The custom has grown in popularity and is now considered big business.

Christmas began as a Christian festival, but today it is also observed to a certain extent by some Jews. They send presents and cards to their friends.

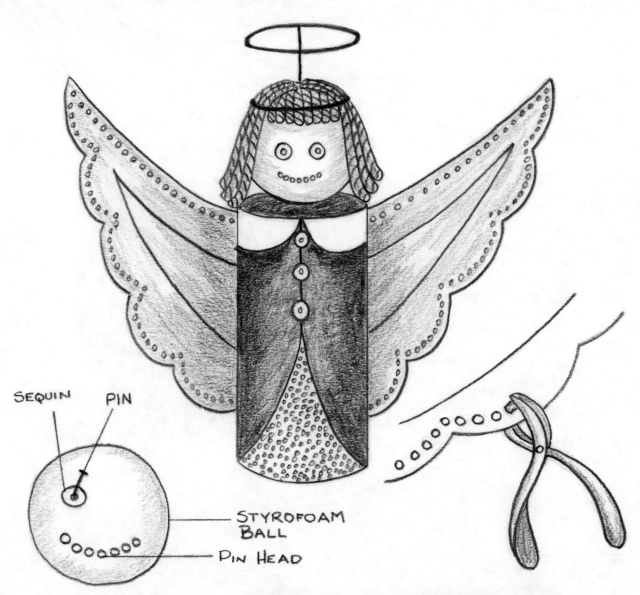

SEQUIN   PIN

STYROFOAM
BALL

PIN HEAD

ANGELS ALL

Use cardboard center of tissue roll as the body of the angel. Garment is made of colored construction paper and is glued to the roll. Cut wings from aluminum foil. Punch holes as shown in the illustration to decorate wings. Sequins may also be glued on. Cut slots in cardboard center and insert wings. Stuff center with newspaper and glue on styrofoam ball as head. Colored rope or ribbons are used for the hair. Eyes may be small buttons or other suitable material.

SPECIAL ORNAMENTS

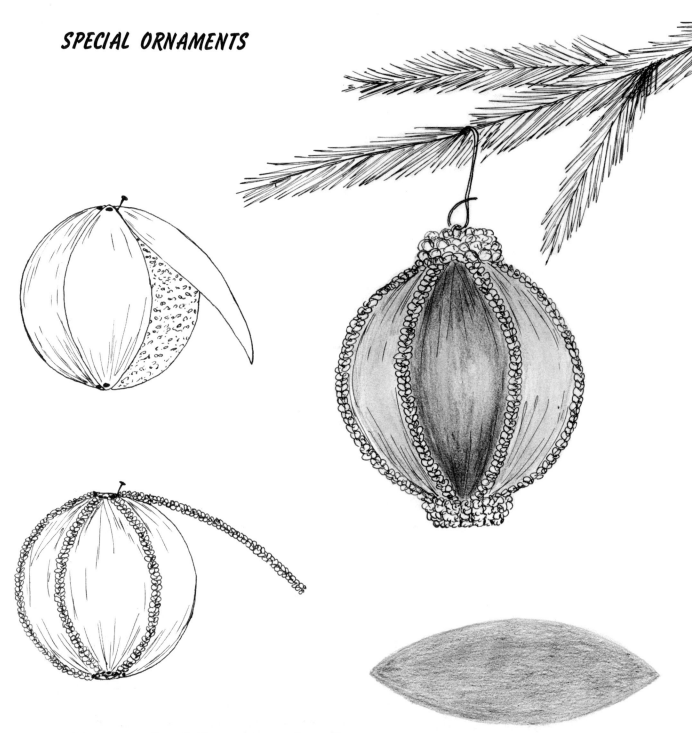

Using a styrofoam ball, cut six strips that will cover the surface of the ball. Glue in place with white glue. At the joints, glue strip of decorative binding, add hair pin or paper clip for attachment.

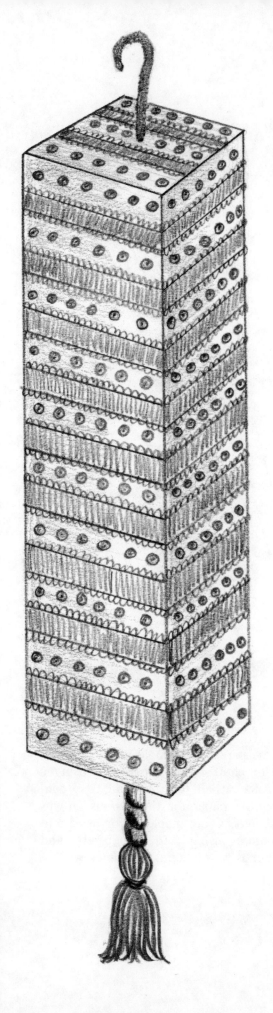

ALL FROM CONTAINERS

Toothpaste boxes, mailing tubes and tissue paper tubes can be used. Glue on ends and spray with spray paint. When dry use glue and braid, glitter and sequins. Use pipe cleaners for hangers. Add your own decorative touch to these unique ornaments.

THREE WISE MEN

These paper cup people are made from six or eight ounce paper cups using a styrofoam ball for the head. Use construction paper for the various crowns and hats. Glue on paper for arms and decorate using sequins, beads and glitter as your imagination dictates.

182

PSYCHEDELIC SPHERES

Cut a series of circles from heavy cardboard with a small cut halfway through each one. Join the two spheres together as illustrated. Permit to dry and then decorate with various colors in a modernistic way. Sequins and glitter may be added on both the front surfaces and edges. A loop of string is glued at the joint to provide for hanging. Make a dozen or so and use a small spotlight to highlight them as they hang on the tree.

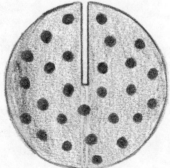

Attach three different size styrofoam balls to one another, working from the base up from the largest to the smallest. These balls can be attached using a round toothpick. The features can be sequins attached with small pins. The arms are from pipe cleaners and small buttons are used to simulate coat buttons. The hat is constructed from black construction paper and glued into place. The base is flattened to provide stability by using a knife to cut off that portion as necessary. Clothing such as tie, scarf, and so on, may be added by using small bits of material.

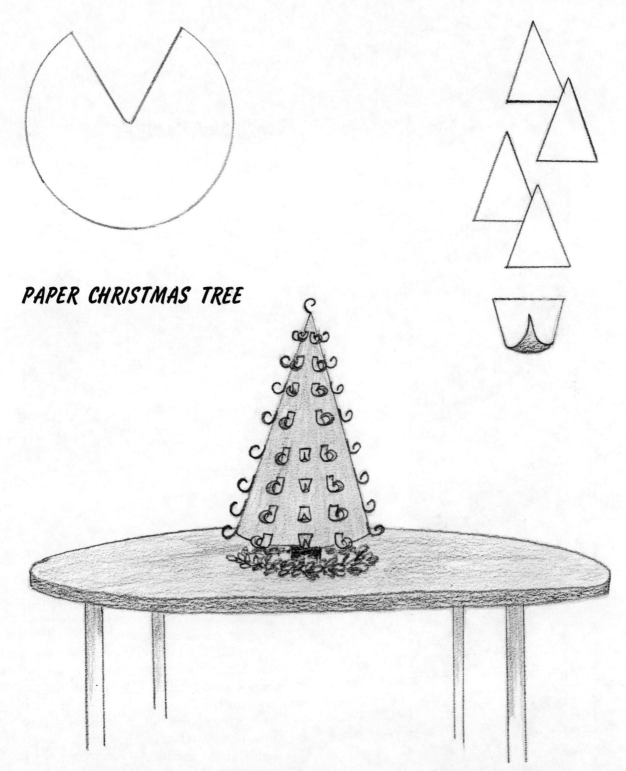

PAPER CHRISTMAS TREE

A large circle at least eighteen inches in diameter is cut out of a heavy piece of construction paper. A small shaped area is removed from this circle. The two sections are joined together forming a large cone. To the outside of this cone are glued many small pieces of coiled bits of various colored construction paper simulating the leaves on a tree. These pieces of paper are best cut in a triangular shape with the narrow end of the triangle coiled as illustrated.

185

HOLIDAY CANDLES

Use a four to six inch heavy cardboard tube, generally the type that is used as the center support for rolled rugs, and the like. This tube is painted all white with spray paint and a red two inch ribbon is wound in a helical fashion from top to bottom. The ends of this ribbon are glued. The base is a twelve inch by twelve inch piece of ¾ inch pine. A circle disk is cut and glued just inside the top to hold a light socket. An electrical cord is attached to the socket, brought down through the center and a small groove cut in the base with a plug attached to the end. These units can be made in virtually any size to suit the individual needs.

The stained glass look is from mosaics made from colored paper that has been cut into strips and fitted together. Trim outside intertriangles and frame using stiff cardboard as a border. The gentle overlap of each color by gluing joints provides the effect of lead.

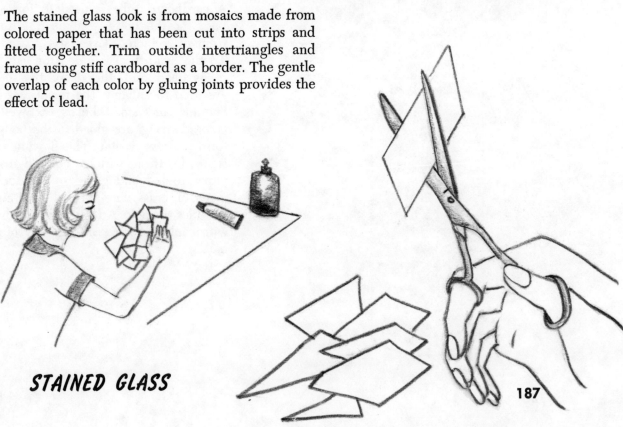

STAINED GLASS

187

MY OWN ANGEL

A cardboard tube is used to form the base for the body. The head is made from a two inch or larger styrofoam ball. To the head yarn is glued for hair. Sequins, beads and other decorative means are used to enhance the facial features. Sequins and small beads, as well as colored string, are glued to the body to form a dress design. The flowing robe is made from various colored tissue paper folded and glued to the top. A piece of brass wire formed in a circle provides the halo. Attach under the head with each end stuck into the styrofoam ball.

188

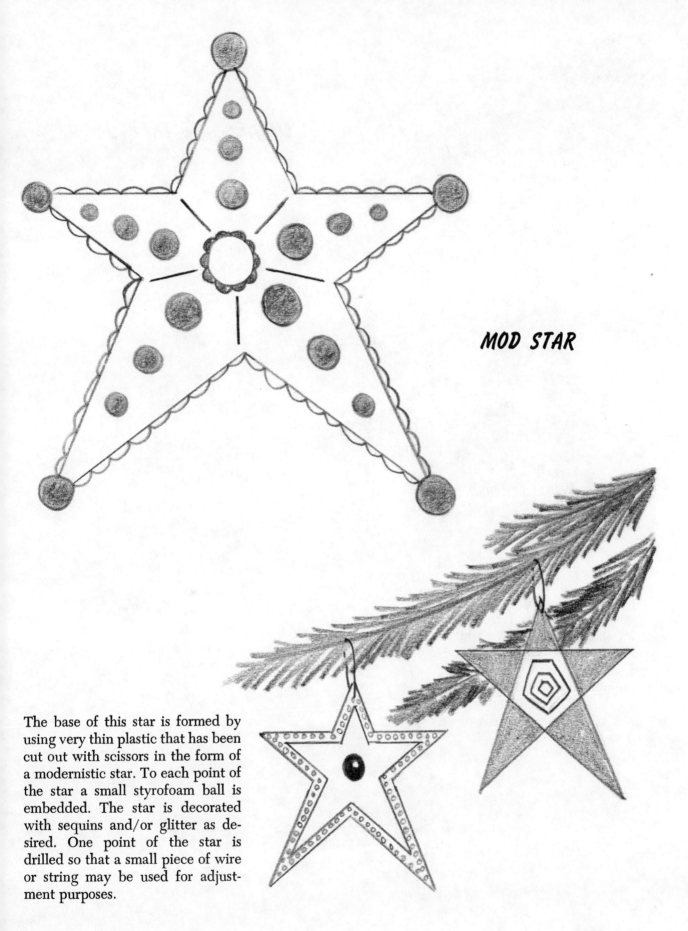

MOD STAR

The base of this star is formed by using very thin plastic that has been cut out with scissors in the form of a modernistic star. To each point of the star a small styrofoam ball is embedded. The star is decorated with sequins and/or glitter as desired. One point of the star is drilled so that a small piece of wire or string may be used for adjustment purposes.

Sugar cones (ice cream) form the bases for these unique units. Add decorative touches with ribbon, colored string, lace, sequins and glitter. Tempera paints may also be used to enhance and individualize each unit. Attach thread to apex of cone for hanging.

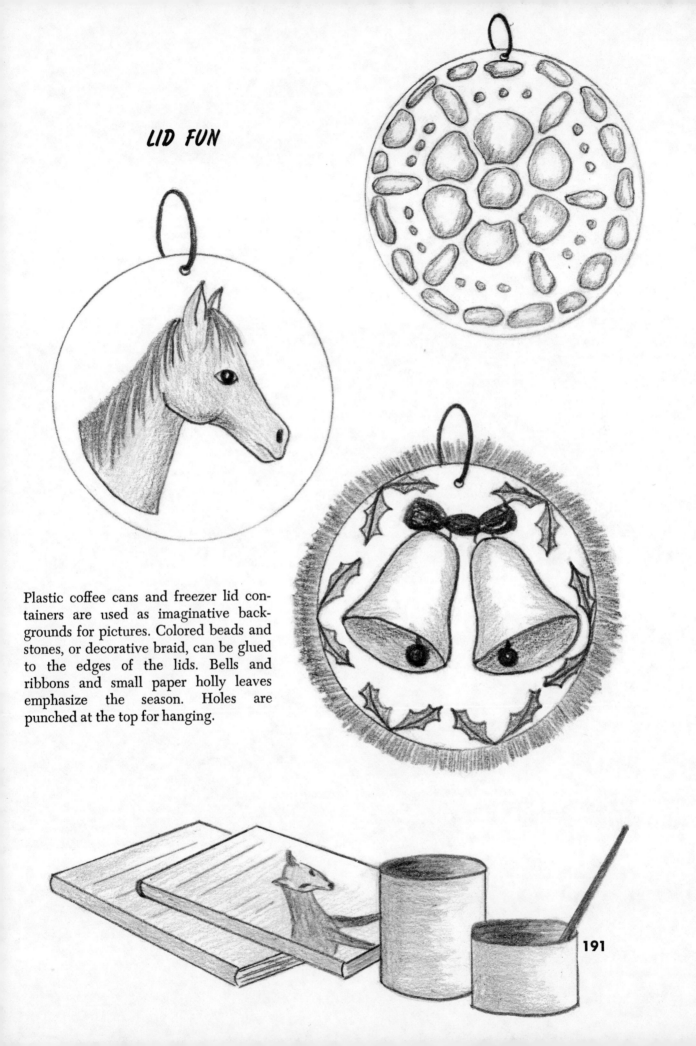

LID FUN

Plastic coffee cans and freezer lid containers are used as imaginative backgrounds for pictures. Colored beads and stones, or decorative braid, can be glued to the edges of the lids. Bells and ribbons and small paper holly leaves emphasize the season. Holes are punched at the top for hanging.

191